Dyer D. Lum

The Spiritual Delusion

Its methods, teachings, and effects: the philosophy and phenomena critically

examined

Dyer D. Lum

The Spiritual Delusion

Its methods, teachings, and effects: the philosophy and phenomena critically examined

ISBN/EAN: 9783337239633

Printed in Europe, USA, Canada, Australia, Japan

Cover: Foto ©Thomas Meinert / pixelio.de

More available books at **www.hansebooks.com**

THE "SPIRITUAL" DELUSION;

Its Methods, Teachings, and Effects.

THE PHILOSOPHY AND PHENOMENA CRITICALLY EXAMINED.

BY

DYER D. LUM,

AUTHOR OF "THE EARLY SOCIAL LIFE OF MAN."

." 'Tis an unweeded garden
That grows to seed; things rank and gross in nature
Possess it merely."
HAMLET.

PHILADELPHIA:
J. B. LIPPINCOTT & CO.
1873.

Entered according to Act of Congress, in the year 1873, by
J. B. LIPPINCOTT & CO.,
In the Office of the Librarian of Congress at Washington.

TO

THE MEMORY

OF

MY BROTHER AND SISTER,

THIS ATTEMPT TO RESCUE THE NAMES OF OUR LOVED ONES BEYOND THE SILENT RIVER
AND THE TENDER MEMORIES ASSOCIATED WITH THEM TREASURED IN THE
SECRET RECESSES OF OUR HEARTS, FROM PROFANATION
BY STROLLING JUGGLERS AND THEIR
CREDULOUS DUPES,

THESE PAGES
ARE AFFECTIONATELY DEDICATED.

PREFACE.

IN presenting this little work to the public, it may be well to state at the outset that no new theory is urged to account for the "spiritual manifestations" so loudly asserted to be everywhere occurring, nor is it designed to definitely map out the causes of all the phenomena presented by "mediums" with the accuracy of a phrenological chart.

While not assuming to offer anything *new* on this well-worn subject, it has seemed to the author that an examination of the claim of the spiritists, that disembodied fellow-mortals do communicate and manifest themselves to us, might commend itself to many still halting in their convictions with regard to these singular phenomena. That they are not the result of spiritual beings operating from the unseen may be definitely shown; and to group together the various reasons leading to this conclusion, to show that the phenomena in question do not require the presence of hypothetical "spirits," is the aim of the following pages.

In the consideration of the subject, many phenomena that, owing to their marvelousness, commend themselves to the simple as "demonstrative evidences" of the spirital theory, will be seen to be explicable upon scientific principles; a less number, vociferously asserted to be "tests," may not be so easily explained; but even in these cases we may clearly see that "spirits" are in no event to be accredited with their occurrence.

To those who have neither the time nor inclination to thoroughly investigate the subject in the light of modern scientific research, but are still perplexed with the apparent mystery surrounding it, these pages are addressed, the author believing that a statement of the reasons which have led him out of this treacherous quicksand to healthful moral action may be of service to many not as yet lost to all appeals to reason and common sense.

NORTHAMPTON, MASS., May, 1873.

CONTENTS.

PART I.

THE PHILOSOPHY.

CHAPTER I.

MODERN SPIRITISM UNSCIENTIFIC IN ITS METHODS.

                                                                   PAGE

1. In its recurrence to savage modes of thought 9
2. In its implicit denial of uniformity in nature 13
3. In its investigations based on assumption 16
4. In its reliance on unsatisfactory testimony and unwarranted inferences 22
5. In its bizarre contributions to scientific knowledge 25

CHAPTER II.

MODERN SPIRITISM UNPHILOSOPHICAL IN ITS TEACHINGS.

1. In its materialistic spiritualism 42
2. In its confusion of distinctions between physical and spiritual realms of being 51
3. In its claim of higher spirituality for rejuvenated polytheism... 56
4. In its fallacious mental philosophy 76

CHAPTER III.

MODERN SPIRITISM UNNATURAL IN ITS EFFECTS.

1. In its effect on mental health by destroying self-reliance 80
2. In its effect on spiritual health by fostering superstition 85
3. In its effect on physical health by developing abnormal faculties... 92
4. In its effect on moral health by weakening self-control 94

PART II.

THE PHENOMENA.

CHAPTER I.

	PAGE
INTRODUCTORY	99

CHAPTER II.

MENTAL EXALTATION.

1. In mental derangement 104
2. In the use of stimulants 107
3. In slumber 111
4. In magnetic somnolency 114

CHAPTER III.

"OBSESSION."

1. Evidence of the senses 125
2. The witchcraft delusion 129
3. Mental epidemics 138

CHAPTER IV.

UNCONSCIOUS ACTION OF THE BRAIN.

1. Unconscious cerebration 148
2. All impressions permanent 157
3. Mental telegraphing and prevision 164

CHAPTER V.

"WHAT PHENOMENA OCCUR?"

1. Liability to self-delusion 182
2. Tendency of scientific research 195

CHAPTER VI.

PHYSICAL MANIFESTATIONS.

1. Involuntary actions 205
2. Hints towards a solution 226

THE "SPIRITUAL" DELUSION.

PART I.—THE PHILOSOPHY.

CHAPTER I.

MODERN SPIRITISM UNSCIENTIFIC IN ITS METHODS.

1. *In its recurrence to savage modes of thought.*

LIVING in a barbarous and unlettered condition, the sport of conflicting forces alternately fostering and destroying the fruit of his labors, and exciting fear and trembling by the apparent waywardness of their action, the savage would naturally seek for some explanation of these confusing phenomena, and the means to avert impending calamities in future.

Trees sheltered him from the burning rays of the sun, and afforded fuel for his fire; fire warmed him when chilled by exposure, and prepared his food in a more palatable manner; beasts clothed him, and could be made useful in many ways; water not only slaked his thirst, but also cleansed his body; rains refreshed him, and gave renewed life to vegetation. These facts would call forth no thought from a savage mind. But his rude and selfish consciousness could not but observe that these facts were not always calculated for his benefit, but were apparently controlled by motives as uncertain and contrary as human passions. These unknown forces excited his fears and terrors.

Fire could consume him, water drown him, trees crush him. What the sun had nurtured, storms would destroy. The long and patient labor of multitudes would in a few hours be swept away. Whence came this strange contrariety of actions, so like in its effects to human passions and impulses? Evidently from superior beings, invisible it is true, but whose existence and power were daily seen in the devastating effects they produced.

The explanation thus naturally adopted would be resorted to whenever any event transcended his limited range of experience. "Animism," says E. B. Tylor, "is the doctrine of all men who believe in active spiritual beings; it is essentially the antagonist of materialism, and in some form or other it is the religion of mankind, from the rude savage of the Australian bush or the Brazilian forest, up to the most enlightened Christian. Now, animism in the lower civilization is not only a religion, but also a philosophy; it has to furnish rational explanations of one phenomenon after another, which we treat as belonging to biology or physics. If a man is alive and moving, the animistic explanation is, that the soul, a thin, ethereal, not immaterial being, in the man's likeness, is within him, animating him, just as one gets inside a coat and moves it. If the man sleeps and dreams, then either the soul has gone out of him to see sights which he will remember when he wakes, or it is lying quiet in his body, receiving visits from the spirits of other people, dead or alive,—visits which we call dreams. If a man, when fasting or sick, sees a vision, this is a ghost or some other spirit; if he faints or falls into a fit, his soul has gone out from him for a time, and must be recalled with mystic ceremonies; if it returns, he recovers, but if it stays away permanently, then the man is dead. If the man takes a fever or goes mad, then it is a spirit which is hovering about the person, shaking or maltreating him, or it has got inside him, and is driving him, tearing him, speaking and crying by his voice."

This description of savage thought is not without its parallel in our own land of boasted civilized thought. Instead of any reference to physical cause and effect, the spiritist hastily assumes the presence and agency of a "spirit," to account for phenomena which transcend the powers of his mind. Assuming a learned look, the spiritist seeks to confute "groveling, mole-eyed science" by an elaborate collection of the superstitious rites and observances of uncivilized tribes of men, to *demonstrate* the universality of commerce with spiritual beings, seemingly unconscious that by thus allying himself with rope-tying Greenland angekoks, Ojibway conjurers, and Siberian shamans, he is virtually confessing antagonism to the spirit of science, and seeking to restore the philosophy of ruder and more barbarous times.

Professor Tylor says, "Set a Chinese and an English medium to obtain written missives from the respective spirits they believe in, and let a wild Ojibway Indian look on at the performance. So far as the presence of disembodied spirits goes, possessing the performers, and guiding the pencils, or manifesting themselves by raps, or voices, or other actions, the savage would understand and admit it at once, for such things are part of his recognized system of nature: the only part of the affair out of his line would be the art of writing, which does belong to a higher grade of civilization than his. In a word, a modern medium is a red Indian or a Tartar shaman in a dress-coat."

"If communion be indeed a fact," the spiritist retorts,

"why should not the fact be alike intelligible to all three?" We reply, it is more than a question of fact: it is a question involving the true method of interpreting facts; whether "facts" shall be explained by the savage philosophy or the scientific method. "But if it be a fact?" Oh, most wise and sapient reasoner! If it be indeed a fact that this mode of thought is the true torch to unravel the mysteries of nature, by throwing an instantaneous light on all marvelous phenomena, then the savage was a wise man, and the year 1873 is far down on the scale of decadence, and the sooner we break our crucibles and retorts, the better.

To briefly state the radical difference between these two forms of thought will be sufficient to show that our charge is true and unanswerable. The savage attributes spiritual life as an adequate cause for all uncomprehended events. The belief in fairies, banshees, ghosts, witches, sorcery, etc., is a survival of savage thought, and to science alone are we indebted for emancipation from it. Belief in dreams and visions, as originating in an objective spiritual world, is savage thought; as being subjective phenomena of mind, is scientific. To regard the cataleptic as a medium, is savage philosophy; as a patient, is scientific. To the savage, apparitions are real; science classifies them under well-understood laws, as mental hallucinations. To the savage, every medicine-man, conjurer, or shaman attests his commerce with "spirits" by phenomena consisting in strange noises, rope-tying, and beating of drums by "invisibles." Communion with the unseen thus becomes possible by knocks and the movement of objects. To the student in science, explanation of phenomena based on ignorance of natural causes is emphatically unscientific.

2. *In its implicit denial of uniformity in nature.*

The researches of the astronomer into the boundless expanse of the universe, filled with worlds and systems of worlds; the investigations of the geologist unraveling the history of our planet down through countless cycles of time to primordial fire-mist; the discoveries of the biologist concerning the genesis and evolution of life from its earliest, scarce recognizable form, to its master-piece, the "human form divine," are all the result of the mind having clearly conceived the grand idea of uniformity and law in nature. The philosophy of the past has given way to new methods, under which all events are being slowly grouped as the result of natural causes. Not only in the physical world has the conception of uniformity triumphed, but as well in the world of mind. Dr. Draper, well aware of the intimate connection between man and nature, has remarked that but for the Gulf Stream, Newton would not have written his Principia, nor Milton sung; for (otherwise) England would have been as bleak and dreary as Labrador, and the Anglo-Saxon race mere Esquimaux.

If Washington, Lafayette, Kosciusko, and Kossuth had been born and obliged to live in abject poverty, struggling through life for merely enough to prevent the divorce of soul and body, as millions do, the world would never have heard their eloquent words, or witnessed their still more eloquent deeds. Is not life itself influenced by invariable law? Births and deaths are ever relatively the same, not merely in number, but also in regard to sex. By the study of statistics we may even calculate how many letters without any address will this month be dropped in the Boston post-office, apparently one of the most accidental of events.

The same is true, not only of crime in the aggregate, but even as to its nature, enabling us to determine both the perihelion and aphelion of any crime in its annual orbit. In summer, crimes against persons preponderate over crimes against property; in winter, the reverse. The tendency of women to commit crimes against persons is, to men, the same as the relations of physical strength between the two sexes. We cannot assert of this man or of that that he will commit a crime, yet we ascertain the relative number of each given offense that will be committed during the year in any country not disturbed by exceptional exciting events.

It is only by taking in a wider field of vision, a more enlarged retrospect of human action, that uniformity becomes apparent. Yet of individual human action, it must be borne in mind, we can form no definite estimate, nor predetermine an act.

The spiritist theoretically affirms the universality of law, but practically denies it by introducing new factors to still more complicate the mystery; and these unknown factors being "spirits," they are not amenable to the laws of matter and motion on our terrestrial sphere, but override or annul them at will.

Our knowledge of the uniformity in the aggregate actions of men results from our having abundant means to examine these actions, from the most trivial to the most important. Spiritist literature is replete with anecdotes illustrating the power of "spiritual beings" to suspend the natural order of things to avert some personal calamity. "Spirits" have been known, it is soberly asseverated, to stop the water-wheel of a mill without the use of the lever; to cause persons *to fall* up hill when destruction would have awaited their downward course. They interfere in all the domestic relations of this world to thwart or aid our plans and accomplish their ends, however whimsical. I have heard a—so-called—"well-attested" instance of a gentleman lying in his bed in the morning and hearing "spirits" strike a match and light a fire in the stove prepared over-night! Some of our prominent spiritist lecturers wear gold charms said to have been brought to them " by spiritual agency." The question where *they* got them is not pressed!

Science is based on the universality of law; and to assert that " spirits " are controlled by law does not evade the charge, for, from the very nature of the case, it must be by laws governing their world or condition of existence, not ours, and consequently beyond the grasp of our faculties here, for the evident reason that we are unable to obtain any glimpse of that condition of life, save what is occasionally reflected through " mediumship." As long as we are unable to observe the "spirits" in their daily and hourly avocations, we can form no conception of the laws governing them, nor of the extent of their power over the physical forces of gravity, light, heat, etc.

The phenomena of individual mental action have not yet been co-ordinated under law, and many philosophers, in fact, all of the school of spiritual philosophy, in affirming the freedom of the will, deny its possibility in individual cases. If, therefore, human will, operating from the unseen, can interfere in all the relations of life, and destroy the apparent connection between cause and effect, then affirmations of law are but empty sound and utterly meaningless. The Greeks recognized the universality of law in the same sense, and when any mysterious event occurred inexplicable to them, it was ascribed to some spiritual being working in accordance with the laws of another sphere of existence.

The crowning glory of science is that it has exorcised

the "spirits" out of the trees and winds, out of the rivers and mountains. Even the later forms of the same phase of thought, regarding forces as mysterious *entities* lying latent in matter, have had to succumb to the power of physical investigation.

A recent writer has aptly remarked, "This broad domain has been conquered little by little; for the spirits have always been very loath to go. They cling longest in the obscurest parts of existence, where it is difficult for the exorcising process to penetrate. They still persist in retaining a certain control of the mental operations; though with most of scientists the mind is placed, with all things else, under the dominion of force and law."

Is it asserted that a knowledge of mind is not included in a knowledge of nature? If so, it is an unproven assumption, and the cause of the barrenness of much metaphysical speculation. The metaphysician, with his deductions from pure reason, and the theologian, with his Thus saith the—— anything but proven facts, have been tried and found incompetent to decide the phenomena of mind, and upon scientists has the task descended. But modern science, we are sometimes warned, is materialistic! Names or epithets have lost their power, happily, in deterring us from investigation. We are first to ask, not where or to what does a principle lead, but, Is it true? Is it based on facts?

3. *In its investigations based on assumption.*

Scientific investigation is based on a careful and scrutinizing accumulation of facts, until it becomes possible to rise to some generalization and grasp the law underlying them. "Spirit," says Sir David Brewster, "is the last thing I shall give in to;" and he was right; for, the hypothesis once granted, investigation for critical purposes ceases; inquiry for the *cause* is no longer needed when the phenomenon, moreover, occurs in that realm of which he possesses the least accurate knowledge concerning its nature and hidden springs of action, the clear conception of uniformity, that has never as yet failed him in his elucidation of nature's mysteries, renders him loath to recur to savage forms of thought for an explanation.

He rather queries within himself, "I am as yet ignorant of the workings of the human mind in too many respects to hastily indorse the spirital hypothesis. We know that in former times it was believed most where natural law was understood least: thus patron saints manifested themselves to Catholic believers, fairies and elves to those who had no doubt of their existence, and devils admitted they were obsessing and bewitching mortals when addressed by orthodox interrogators.* The interrelation of forces in the domain of psychological science is as yet too little understood; there seems to remain too much room for inference that the mind, though altogether unconsciously, may have much to do with the shaping of these purported communications I must investigate not only the phenomena, but the mental status

---

* " The Greeks and Romans of antiquity were just as much liable to disorders of the nervous system as we are, but to them supernatural appearances came under mythologic forms,—Venus, and Mars, and Minerva. The places of these were taken in the dreams of the ascetics of the Middle Ages by phantoms of the Virgin and the saints. At a still later time, in Northern Europe, and even in England, where the old pagan superstitions are scarcely yet rooted out of the vulgar mind, even though the Reformation has broken the system of ecclesiastical thought, fairies and brownies and Robin Goodfellow survive. The form of phantoms has changed with change of the creed of communities, and we may therefore, with good Reginald Scot, inquire, 'If the apparitions which have been seen by true men and brave men in all ages of the world were real existences, what has become of the swarms of them in these latter times?'"—Draper's *Human Physiology*, p. 407.

2*

of the medium through whom these so-called revelations come, before I can decide as to their origin."

The scientist ascribes any given phenomenon, when the cause is unknown, to the operation of some natural law,— to laws operative here, not to laws peculiar to the spheres, —and never loses sight of this in his attempts to investigate. If a table moves, it must be by the application of *force;* in what manner it is applied, and the nature of the force, is the problem to be worked out. If scientists had ever lost sight of this aim in their researches, our knowledge of nature would be naught.

When the Greeks first observed the singular phenomenon of electricity induced by rubbing amber, even the philosophers were amazed and marveled much. Investigation but deepened their conviction that some "external influence" was there manifesting itself, and they sapiently concluded that minute spirits dwelt in the amber, who, becoming exasperated, threw out their feelers and claws to seize whatever came in contact with them.* "Spirit-influence" thus coming in, the very pos-

---

* "It is an opinion of the remotest antiquity, that there exists nothing, however vile and abject, no disease of the mind, no virtue, that is not under the protection and control of some particular demon or genius. The doctrine is said to have been derived originally from the Chaldeans. Be this as it may, one thing is unquestionable, and evident, even from the authority of Hesiod, that the earliest inhabitants of Greece were imbued with it; and it is no less certain that the opinion was propagated from the people to the professors of wisdom themselves, having been adopted by Pythagoras and Plato, philosophers of the highest authority. With respect to Plato, indeed, no one can doubt that, if the philosophy which he taught his disciples be divested of the doctrine of demons and genii, it loses its most important part. And how prone Pythagoras was to enlarge the empire of demons, may be learned both from many other incidents in his history, and especially from the fact that he at once referred to them the causes of all recondite and abstruse matters. Being asked what occasioned the acute sound emitted from brass, he gravely

sibility of scientific explanation vanished, and we had to wait two thousand years for the electric telegraph.

With many spiritists, investigation in any true sense of the word is impossible. By far the larger portion of them having but the most limited knowledge of psychological phenomena, more particularly of disordered intellectual or sensitive action, the marvelousness of the phenomenon in question is sufficient to elicit their full credence in its super-physical origin. Even ordinary cases of imperfect mental action are often sufficient to convince them that they are the result of *mediumship*. So completely does this preconception control the ardent spiritist, that if a table tips, or crockery breaks, no step can be taken towards an "investigation" until a *medium* has been sent for to ascertain what the assumed "spirit" wants, or who he or she is. Does a person manifest strange nervous action; "investigation" first of all requires that a *circle* be formed! Do certain involuntary movements of the muscles occur; a "spirit" is endeavoring to "manifest"!

Dr. Wigan, in his "Duality of the Mind" (pages 237–9), cites the case of a young man of distinction, and good disposition, who was "influenced" by an uncontrollable desire to run up into the organ-loft during divine service, and play some well-known jocular tune, and frequently one of an indecent character. He always appeared sorry for it, and declared that he used every exertion to prevent it, but in vain, and finally had to ab-

---

replied that it was the voice of a demon shut up in the brass!"—Porphyrius, De Vita Pythagor., p. 42. Who would have expected such an answer from a geometrician? And yet what method can be more convenient and expeditious than this, towards clearing away all the difficulties which beset those who investigate the causes of things?"—Mosheim's Notes on Cudworth, vol. ii. p. 264.

stain entirely from public service, though he would read the prayers at home with apparently sincere and tranquil devotion. If he accidentally passed an open church-door, the temptation was irresistible, and often resulted in serious embarrassment to him. In all other respects he was perfectly sane, but was subject to periodical epileptic fits.

In our midst, such a case would excite no surprise in the mind of the spiritist : he would see therein a convincing " manifestation of obsession." His theory would lead him to have the young man's mediumistic powers more fully developed, that " spirits" of a higher grade might be enabled to control him ; or by magnetic passes and kind words of advice seek to quiet the restless " influence." The scientist would see in the young man, not a *medium* to be developed, but a patient requiring treatment, and if he sent for any one it would be for his physician. He would seek to restore the young man to a state of health, rather than " develop" a disordered state of the brain into irrecoverable madness, or a more fatal result.

This illustration is given here, not as a type of what is known as " spirit-control," but to illustrate the diverse methods by which the scientist and spiritist would be governed in their treatment of the case. The scientist is habituated to co-ordinating facts first, and then seeking to grasp the law underlying them. The one investigates to discover the cause, the other to obtain a " test" to indorse his preconceived views. In the case given above, the scientist concludes it is imperfect mental action, because similar cases are of not unfrequent occurrence where this can alone explain them, and he has been led by a large collection of facts to associate the presence of epileptic fits with imperfect mental action ; whilst to the spiritist, the epileptic paroxysms, if not viewed as additional evidence of "obsession," would be regarded as extraneous to it.

In any circle for "physical manifestations," who ever heard of spiritists investigating the connection between the mental powers of the medium and the intelligence evinced in the manifestations? In a circle for "musical manifestations," for instance, the spiritist investigator takes great pains to see that the *medium* is securely bound, and that no movement can be made without his knowledge; and then, if the piano plays, or the guitar floats in the room, he is satisfied it is the work of "spirits," *because* he knows the *medium* has not touched an instrument!

Do they ever seek to ascertain whether the compositions played by the "influence" are familiar or not to the mind of the *medium*? Do they ever question whether the information obtained is such as to be new to all present? Do they ever call for some tune they know to be unknown to the *medium* or never heard by him? Ropes and bandages have no effect on the exercise of mental faculties, and the readiness with which they are relied on is evidence of the unfitness of the spiritist to conduct a scientific investigation. He is too much concerned in maintaining the requisite "conditions" insisted upon by the *medium*, to press any question: instead of preparing tests, he is seeking them.

I well remember the first "spiritual séance" I ever attended. Many years since, in Springfield, Massachusetts, I was invited to attend a "test-circle" held for the purpose of investigation. The *medium* was a Dr. McFadden, a smooth-tongued and stoutly-built gentleman, wearing his hair in long oily ringlets. We all clasped hands in a circle composed of about a dozen individuals; the "doctor" said it was necessary to have a lady sit on each side of him, as ladies were "negative" and he possessed too much "positivism." On no account, we were charged, were we to withdraw our hands and break the chain of magnetic attraction. Twice through forgetfulness, some one removed a hand from a neighbor's, and each time the "doctor" fell back with his head on the breast of one of the ladies beside him, giving vent to several groans, as if he had received a severe shock. Anxious to introduce a private test of my own, I slyly loosed my hold on the hand of the person next me, farthest removed from the *medium*, unknown to him, and, lo! no shock was felt.

We spent two hours in the "investigation," and received one "test." An elderly gentleman in the circle was told that on the side of the great toe of his left foot there was a small mole! The gentleman said he was not aware of it, and the circle broke up, and awaited in breathless expectancy an appeal to the fact. Retiring to one corner, the gentleman proceeded to ascertain if the statement was correct, and informed us that the "doctor" was right. This was glory enough for one night; and in the midst of the general congratulations of the faithful, I deposited my fifty-cent scrip in the medium's ready hat, and departed to muse over my first lesson in the "spiritual philosophy of the nineteenth century."

This is an actual fact, and related without exaggeration, and I have no doubt that any who have met the "doctor" in his peregrinations will instantly recognize its inherent probability.

4. *In its reliance on unsatisfactory testimony and unwarranted inferences.*

The mere fact that certain phenomena occur without visible human agency is regarded as irrefutable evidence of immortality! Not to recapitulate what has already been said, we charge spiritism with being unscientific in its reliance on inferences drawn from a certain class of phenomena as related in the columns of the spiritual press. These testimonies as published can furnish no ground for conviction, nor basis for examination. The innumerable points which, as we have seen, pass by unnoticed or are regarded as extraneous by the narrator often contain the key to solve the whole mystery.

In the case related in the last section, as narrated by Dr. Wigan, we found especial prominence given to the all-important fact of epilepsy. But if the same case had been narrated by a spiritist for the columns of one of his journals, he would not have felt the same necessity for mentioning it, and might have omitted all reference to it in his testimony.

The state of mind that can greedily devour the ill-digested narrations of events transpiring in what is known in spiritual nomenclature as the "night-side of nature," or the "debatable land," is the very reverse of that brought to bear upon scientific problems. The spiritist, if a medium, is completely under the control of the dominating idea, and is incapable of prosecuting a critical inquiry. Dr. Carpenter, in his "Human Physiology" (p. 633), truly observes, "When the mind has once yielded itself up to the dominance of these erroneous ideas, they can seldom be dispelled by any process of reasoning; for it results from the very nature of the previous habits of thought that the reasoning-powers are weakened, and that the volitional control, through want of exercise, can no longer be exerted. If an attempt be made to reason a patient out of a delusion by demonstrating its complete inconsistency with the most obvious facts, the reply will be generally something to this effect: 'I have stronger evidence than anything which *you* can urge,—the evidence of *my own* feelings.'"

Have you seen wonderful things? publish it to the world; collect a mass of testimony written under preconceived conceptions, and by its weight crush out all cavil and doubt. Does a man float in the air? *therefore* he is immortal! Does a man in Portland, with a broken back, spin around upon the foot-board of the bed on the injured part, like a tee-totum? *therefore* "thou shalt never die"! Do "spirits" in Montpelier lift cats in the air by the tail with invisible hands? *therefore* thy relatives and friends are ever with thee! Can a *medium* in Boston tell me what I knew before, or how much change I have in my pocket, which I did not know? "O death, where is thy sting? O grave, where is thy victory?" Science is hardly prepared to resign to conjecture, and the question *does* become pertinent, "What phenomena occur?"

Professor Tyndall, with much force, has said, "The present promoters of spiritual phenomena divide themselves into two classes, one of which needs no demonstration, while the other is beyond the reach of proof. The victims like to believe, and they do not like to be undeceived. Science is perfectly powerless in the presence of this frame of mind. It is, moreover, a state perfectly compatible with extreme intellectual subtlety and capacity for devising hypotheses which only require the hardihood engendered by strong conviction or by callous mendacity to render them impregnable. The logical feebleness of science is not sufficiently borne in mind. It keeps down the weed of superstition, not by logic, but by slowly rendering the mental soil unfit for its cultivation. When science appeals to uniform experience, the spiritualist will retort, 'How do you know that a uniform experience will continue uniform? You tell me that the sun has risen for six thousand years: that is no proof that it will rise to-morrow; within the next twelve hours it may be puffed out by the Almighty.' Taking this ground, a man may maintain the story of 'Jack and the Bean-stalk' in the face of all the science in the world. You urge in vain that science has given us all the knowledge of the universe which we now possess, while spiritualism has added nothing to that knowledge. The drugged soul is beyond the reach of reason. It is in vain that impostors are exposed, and the special demon cast out. He has but slightly to change his shape, return to his house, and find it empty, swept, and garnished." —*Fragments of Science*, p. 409.

5. *In its bizarre contributions to scientific knowledge.*

The progress of science has not been a peaceful one, but rather that of a conquering army, passing victoriously from one battle-field only to find the enemy securely intrenched in another quarter. The strength of science lies in its methods of investigation. Determined to know more of the many mysteries with which we are surrounded, men of science realize that the mind must be divested of all preconceived conclusions on the subject, and pursue the inductive method of collecting a sufficient number of facts before attempting any generalization; to rise from the effect to an understanding of the law by which it is governed, is the method of science.

Long and arduously have men of science labored; with patient and pains-taking toil have they sought to obtain from the clutch of nature a glimpse, however faint, into the great secret; and now, through their labors, we find the conditions of life ameliorated, the comforts, and luxuries even, placed within the reach of the toiling multitudes, and a broader and more comprehensive education generally diffused.

Science has trod no "royal road" to knowledge, but struggled on in thorny paths, bravely trampling difficulties under foot, and ever pressing on, accumulating facts before theories. No guardian "intellectual guide" was there for Watt, or Fulton, or Stephenson, to consult for information in his darkest hour. No familiar stood ready, upon the payment of a certain amount of good and lawful currency, to appear and solve the problems perplexing the mind of Morse, when he was struggling to give form to the idea dimly burning in his brain.

Geologists were content to descend into quarry-beds, and to ascend precipitous mountains, hammer in hand, that they might read but a line on a page of the mighty volume spread out before them. Astronomers were satisfied if mechanical ingenuity could give them a clearer vision of the countless orbs which had so long kept their secret from human eyes, hoping to gain a deeper insight into the laws governing the universe. The biologist knew no greater pleasure than studying his science by the only method that as yet he knew to be capable of producing useful results,—that of careful investigation,—trusting to obtain but a glimpse into that mightiest of all problems,—the problem of problems,—life.

But old things have passed away, and all methods are new, under the light of the New Dispensation. Geologists are no longer required to content themselves with long and arduous toil to read the history of the earth's formation. Sitting in his study, and placing his mind in a condition of "passive receptivity," the geologist may become the agent of another,—of one who has risen above the "cramping influence of material environments" to the full realization of spirital manhood; of one who has a thousand facilities at his command for investigating nature, and libraries far older and more extensive than that of Alexandria at his service, libraries incapable of destruction. He has had it in his power to question the sages of the past, resting after their various reincarnations, and commune with the eminent geologists who have passed on after a lifetime of study. This more extended field of research exhausted, he hastens to unfold the mysteries of nature to the patient toilers in the form, who are still laboriously pursuing the "mole-eyed" method.

Is this a jest? Not at all. The mind of "passive receptivity" having been found (and the spiritists' ranks contain many such), Professor Lyon returns, and presents to mortals, still held in the "cramping influence of material environments," the results of his studies in the higher spheres. The "material" consideration having been satisfactorily arranged to the publisher's notion, "The Hollow Globe" is born, and secrets which have long puzzled the mundane physicist stand revealed. By a trifling outlay of currency the whole mystery of world-building may be ascertained, and "mole-eyed science" forever silenced.

Worlds are made by, or through the agency of, spiritual architects, who frame and fashion the whole material creation after certain immutable laws. And they builded wiser than we knew; for anxious, as we may conjecture, to economize in the expenditure of force, instead of a globe filled with a molten mass and pent-up forces, the earth was made in the form of a hollow globe, and fitted, internal as well as external, for the development of life. According to this new revelation, Lyell was led by his aforesaid "mole-eyed" mistress into many absurdities, calculated to cause a ghost of a smile to flit over the etherealized countenances of the supernal scientists; and Symmes stands revealed as the true prophet of geological science.

"Symmes's Hole" was no imaginative illusion, but a veritable fact, and exists still, awaiting the arrival of the adventuresome explorer, in the vast undiscovered continent, replete with life and tropical vegetation, which, as we know from other Flashes of Light from the Spirit-World, lies in the immediate vicinity of the North Pole! Oh, where is the daring Stanley, to penetrate through the icy barriers surrounding that undiscovered continent, and traverse its smiling valleys and cross its lofty mountains, and bring to us news of Sir John Franklin and his companions? Perhaps the knight has entered that "Hole" into which the Gulf Stream flows, and been borne to happier climes, where he may have renewed the vigor of his youth and be dwelling peacefully.

To all lovers of true science, who have felt a natural repugnance to climb the rocky road and learn the barbarous nomenclature prescribed by Old Science, we commend this volume. No one can doubt its mediumistic origin after one careful perusal, for it bears on every page irrefutable evidence of *not* being the work of any *living* scientist!

Astronomers also may dispense with their instruments, and enjoy a social chat with the inhabitants of the various planets, who occasionally penetrate our atmosphere on tours of scientific investigation. Denizens of the moon visit us, and by their presence confute the theory that their former abode is a burnt-out world, and from their lips we have a vivid description of lunar life and manners on the hither side of the moon's surface.

Certain recent speculations of astronomers, who have confined themselves to the old methods of inductive research, are regarded from the spirital stand-point as fruitful instances of the inherent falsity of their methods, being in direct contradiction with the testimony of the "spirits" who have resided in the sun and the planets, as well as the "evidence" derived from the seer's clear vision of those abodes. Are not persons who have lived on the sun more reliable than mere inferences drawn from spectrum analysis discoveries as to the physical constitution of the sun?

Recent researches of mortal astronomers have led them to conclusions regarding the physical constitution of the major planets of a startling nature; various singular appearances presented by them have led to the supposition that these planets themselves are still intensely heated, and emit light and heat of their own. True, as we know from the pen of A. J. Davis, "in the *beginning* the univercœlum was one boundless, undefinable, unimaginable ocean of Liquid Fire;" but "progression," we had supposed, was fleeter-footed. According to the late Professor Bond, however, Jupiter shines far more brightly than the reflection of the light falling upon his surface will warrant. Observations taken while Jupiter's satellites were passing its face exhibit these satellites as *black spots* on its surface, their reflected light being inappreciable when compared with that of the planet itself. The belt-zones of Jupiter bear witness to terrific convulsions on that planet; the spectrum of Saturn and Uranus, and the nebulous edge presented by the spectrum of Neptune, are thought to be accountable for on no other hypothesis than that these planets have not yet attained that degree of density necessary for the presentation of a solid surface. Hence the major planets are rather to be viewed as secondary suns than as inhabitable worlds; as sources of additional light and heat to their satellites,—rulers of a scheme of subordinate orbs, on which alone the multiform manifestations of life may exist.

But what are sodium lines, when we have direct communication with those who have once lived on these planets? Have we not had duly spread out before us, in the columns of the spiritual press, descriptions of scenery in the Jovian world, and picturesque delineations of the midnight sky on the Saturnian globe? We are told that their inhabitants are far superior to earth's mortals in physical development, and have attained to so high a degree of *spiritual* unfoldment as to be able to pass through the air on their journeys to and fro. They have progressed far beyond earth's sons and daughters, who for countless ages yet to come will not outgrow "the cramping influence of material environments" sufficiently to reach such high *spiritual* attainments. What has secular science told us concerning the seven spheres of the spiritual life? It is to spirital science we owe the grand discovery that they are composed of the *spiritual* emanations constantly emitted by the various planetary bodies.

Without presuming to decide between the rival claims of "spirit-communion" and the "seer's clear vision," as to which is entitled to priority as *evidence*, I will quote briefly from both on this highly important point. Without compromising the authority of our ghostly visitants, we will first refer to the testimony of one who daily visits the "inner life."

"Canst thou form an idea of the magnitude of the second sphere?

"Multiply our earth by twenty-seven million times its present size, and it will give you the *exact size* of *one* of the countless parks of the second sphere.

"How was the spirit-land formed?

"What law was it which formed the sparkling girdles of Saturn? What becomes of the fine invisible particles of matter which emanate from vegetation, from minerals, from all animal bodies, and from the *entire globe*? This earth alone gives off eight hundred million tons of invisible *emanations* every year. Where do these atoms go? The earth *perspires*, like the human body. . . . All the other planets—Mercury, Venus, the vast group of asteroids, Mars, Jupiter, Saturn, the three orbs beyond, together with all their moons [*sic*]—give off fine *emanations* just like the earth. Where do these emanations go? These questions are left you as replies to query as to the foundation of the spirit-land."

The "Milky Way" is composed of countless systems of worlds, of which our solar system is one, and the "second sphere" lies beyond and encircling this. "The second sphere [the spiritual] girdles the first sphere [the "Milky Way"], just as the rings girdle the planet Saturn. The representation is perfect." Thus far from the "clear vision" of Andrew Jackson Davis in "The Present Age and Inner Life," and not, as some may have inferred, from the spirital lips of some ancient Brahmin.

Of all the testimony offered us by the dwellers in the spheres, we will only refer to that given by Immanuel Swedenborg, who in a case of this nature should be deemed a competent judge. That there might be no doubt of the identity of the illustrious Swede, "*twenty spirits*" appeared, and voluntarily took an oath, "in the name of God," that Swedenborg was really present. This distinguished " spirit," having been thus satisfactorily vouched for, deposed as follows: "The second sphere is above the atmosphere, about *six* miles in height. The third occupies about *forty* miles in height. The fourth occupies a still wider space; and so of the others, until the outer boundary of the sixth and commencement of the seventh, which is distant *four* or *five thousand miles.*" "In rising to the spheres, there are *openings* through which we rise."—*Supernal Theology.*

In spiritual geography we have had considerable addition to our fund of knowledge; but, as we are more concerned at present in ascertaining the contributions to mundane science, we leave this highly useful and instructive study, to ascertain in what respects the biologist is indebted to the light of the New Dispensation.

From the *Banner of Light*, of July 6, 1872, I extract from the " Questions and Answers" of the " Banner of Light Free Circles" the following :

" *Question* (from a correspondent).—Among the questions and answers in the *Banner* of December 23d, is opened up a subject of considerable interest, upon which I would be pleased to receive more light from the controlling intelligence. The declaration is made that ' offspring are born to parents in the spirit-world.' Is it supposed or known that the process of generation continues in the higher spheres indefinitely ?

"*Answer* (Theodore Parker).—So far as my experience extends, I learn that the process of generation, so far as the human species is concerned, begins here and ends here; and yet there are spiritual births taking place every hour in our life,—every moment, every second, according to earth-time,—and in this way. *You* are constantly sending off from your life these *germs* that need individualizing, that need to be surrounded by love, by wisdom, and strength, that they may mature in intelligence in the spirit-world. These germs that are thrown off in your life, ere they are ushered into existence here, are destined to an individualized existence in the spirit-world, and they all need fathers and mothers there. They have need of the father's strength to hold them in position until they shall become individualized existence."

There are many questions that might be pressed to elucidate this position of spirital physiology; but I forbear, and leave the "spirit" Theodore Parker to explain in his own way.

"*Ques.*—Please explain what you mean by individualizing the germs thrown off from our own spiritual natures.

"*Ans.*—Gathering to them those elements necessary for form and experience. Your individuality depends upon the amount of elements you have gained from nature. Now, nature extends beyond this earth. It goes through all the spiritual spheres; for without nature there could be no form; without form there could be no experience. Now, these little waifs need assistance in gathering to themselves those elements necessary to build up form,— structures through which the soul can manifest itself and become individualized. When it remains here in the mother-life during the proper time, it gathers these elements from the mother-life. *When it is cast off before the proper time*, it is without these elements; then somebody must assist the little *soul-germ* to gather them for itself. When you feed your infants, you strengthen the form: in the spirit-life they do even more than this; they build up the form. At conception, the soul-germ becomes simply conjoined with matter. Now, then, suppose it is thrown off immediately after that, it is not individualized at all; it is joined to matter, but not individualized. So, then, a mother-life is necessary in the other world,—a mother's love and father's strength. All souls are first conjoined to matter through the sexual relations here in this life, here in the earthly sphere. *That* is the business of this life."

B*

To spirital science we are indebted for new light on "biology;" not the *biology* described in the text-books of the "mole-eyed" system, for spirital science scorns to be indebted to its less ambitious rival, but the "electrical-biology" of the platform, where it is illustrated by its distinguished exponents, "Professor" Stearns, "Professor" Cadwell, and others. Again Mrs. Conant, of Boston, is the medium for this influx of scientific truth, as may be found in the *Banner of Light* for April 6, 1872. Professor Edgar C. Dayton is the ghostly respondent.

"QUESTIONS AND ANSWERS.

"*Question* (from the audience).—Professor Cadwell is in town, giving exhibitions of so-called 'mesmeric' power. After he has slightly manipulated the heads of the persons who present themselves to be mesmerized, they declare that they see any object or scene that he mentions, and, by their actions, indicate that they do believe, for the time being, that they see them. The other evening, besides a variety of other experiments, he caused about a dozen young men apparently to see him boiling coffee on a hot stove, and to snuff up its odor; and when he pretended that he had thrown it on their feet, they pulled off their boots, and jumped about, and acted as if they had been scalded. Yet this pot of coffee and hot stove were nothing but an empty tin cup on a chair, and really nothing had been thrown upon them. . . . I would inquire, 'What is the explanation of these persons seeing scenes and objects which did not exist?'

"*Answer.*—You say he caused them to see scenes which did not exist. I shall be obliged *to take exceptions* to that statement, since all these psychological conditions do exist, of a verity; and they are just as perceptible to the consciousness of the *spiritual senses*, as are conditions

which are apparent to all in this room perceptible to the
consciousness of the material physical senses. Now, when
it is understood that you are all living double lives, that
you possess a double consciousness, one distinct and separate from the other, these things will appear less miraculous. The psychological professor psychologizes his subjects through the action of his spiritual senses. True,
they see no boiling coffee, they physically feel no burn;
and yet, spiritually, this is a positive reality; just as
much a positive reality as it is a positive reality that the
drunkard, during an attack of delirium tremens, sees
snakes and venomous reptiles and they offend him. You
say this is the hallucination of a disordered brain. I say
it is not. There is nothing in all the science of life that
can prove it to be so. It is a *positive, spiritual reality*
to the one who sees, who feels and realizes the condition,
as it is not a reality to one who does not see, feel, and
realize that condition. Now, then, *I deny that there is
any such thing as imagination.* Everything that appeals
to either of our sets of senses, the inner or the outer, is
real, and becomes a demonstrated fact to that one set of
senses at any rate. The others cannot demonstrate it,
because it does not belong to them. . . . The law
of psychology is, properly speaking, the law of spiritual
science.

"*Ques.*—Will you be kind enough to explain just what
you mean by 'psychologizing' a person?

"*Ans.*—I mean this: by bringing them into *rapport* with
your thoughts, with your spiritual senses, your thoughts
act upon these spiritual senses and produce these conditions. For instance: the psychological professor thinks
of boiling coffee; his spiritual senses *inhale* the aroma,
see the boiling coffee, realize the fact. The first thing to
be done is to establish a connection between the two,—

subject and operator. The professor's thoughts act as a key upon his spiritual senses ; in turn, his spiritual senses act in producing these conditions *objectively* to the spiritual senses of the subject. It is almost impossible to clearly elaborate these abstract ideas so that you who are cramped about by mortal conditions can clearly appreciate and understand them."

In the *Banner of Light*, of November 2, 1872, we find Theodore Parker indorsing the same views, and denying the existence of imagination in man. I have taken up so much space with this scientific contribution that I will not pause to comment upon it. In fact, notwithstanding our "cramped conditions," I have no fears but they will be fully "appreciated" by the reader, even though unversed in the rudiments of spiritual science.

To spiritual science we are also indebted for the restoration of astrology to its proper rank in the circle of the sciences, and learned treatises are laid before the public, on the magnetic influence exercised by the planets and fixed stars upon human destiny, and the nature of their influence on the formation of character and personal accountability.

The chemist may break his retorts and discontinue his molecular investigations, and sit at the feet of Theodore Parker, and learn that the accumulation of wealth is a chemical process; for Parker informs us, through the *Banner of Light* (February 11, 1871), of this valuable truth. I submit it in full, that it may receive the attention it merits from students in chemical science :

" That the reception of wealth is indeed a result of the action of chemical laws is an *absolute* truth ; but it is no less true that the chemical relations and conditions of an individual are constantly changing. You are constantly throwing off chemical emanations from your bodies, and taking on new ones. Perhaps to-day you may be *chemically in a fit condition to attract* to yourself wealth,— *gold, silver*, the precious things of this earth. To-morrow you may be chemically another being. Yes; hard work and economy and good common-sense [!] are valuable acquisitions to your chemical condition. They are levers assisting what you have by nature; precisely as a musical education would be of value to one musically endowed by nature. The elements being in the individual, these are conditions that favor their evolutions."

Political economists should seek to thoroughly understand these chemical processes and evolutions!

Spiritists are barred from saying that "spirits" do not enlighten us on scientific subjects, for they have so sought in innumerable cases, or the communications were not from "spirits;" and I think but very few spiritists would hesitate to call Mrs. Conant a veritable *medium*, "through whose organism" most of these facts in spirital science were given. They profess their willingness and ability to receive and answer any question propounded, and yet what *real* addition have we acquired to our fund of practical knowledge? If a scientific question is pressed, we have in reply the merest dribble of "unimaginative" brains, or paltry evasions of facts, by replying in general terms. For instance:

"*Ques.*—Please explain how it is possible that spirits can be photographed.

"*Ans.*—They first pass themselves through a chemical process which is analogous to the process of galvanism. They are plunged—if you please—in a bath of certain chemicals, that will be held in solution for a very short time only, because they are taken from the air, and the air absorbs them again very quickly; but the spirit can hold them in form for a sufficient length of time to impress itself upon the sensitive plate. The use of a medium is necessary as a condenser."—"Theodore Parker," in *Banner of Light*, August 10, 1872.

However much we may object to the lucidity of this *explanation*, we at once see that it professes to grapple the subject. When "mole-eyed science" is found to clash with the teachings of the spirital scientists, no trouble is experienced in solving the difficulty. The following may pass as a sample of the easy method of disposing of such apparent contradictions:

"*Ques.*—I read in the *Banner* that the moon is inhabited by both man and animals. Now, Professor Shaler, of Harvard, and all other scientific men who have made the moon a special study, declare, beyond all doubt, that the conditions necessary to sustain life are not there, nor ever have been. How are we to account for these seemingly flat contradictions?

"*Ans.*—It is very *easy* to account for them. Professor Shaler has not been there; *somebody else has*. One has *absolute* knowledge; the other has guess-work, backed up by a little scientific knowledge,—very poor at that, however. Harvard cannot boast of much!"—"Theodore Parker," in *Banner of Light*, July 27, 1872.

Spiritists object to mundane science that it is "dogmatic" and "one-sided." Not desirous of bandying epithets, I refrain from characterizing the spirit displayed in the above. But Theodore Parker, though evidently a very changed man, was never remarkable in "earth-life" as a scientist, and we therefore part company with him here, to summon Benjamin Franklin on the stand, in whose testimony we should at least expect to observe an absence of dogmatism or self-assertion. Our American philosopher has our spiritual welfare so near his heart that he has assumed control of the editorial portion of the *Banner of Light*,—in other words, is the spirital guide and source of inspiration to the editor thereof, probably supplying the loss of "imagination" in the editorial brain with impressions on the "set of spiritual senses" therein.

In the *editorial* columns of the *Banner of Light*, of October 5, 1872, is an article based on a recent trial of a gentleman (Dr. Schoeppe) for murder through the use of poison. He had been tried and found guilty, but a subsequent trial resulted in his acquittal. Both verdicts were based on the evidence of medical "experts." The philosopher says,—

"In the trial of Mrs. Wharton at Annapolis it was demonstrated, as clearly as it is possible to do it, that science knew no more about matters it considered itself competent to testify upon than ignorance. . . . And now it has come to an equally ignominious end in the case of Dr. Schoeppe, of Pennsylvania. . . . The testimony on the second trial completely destroyed that adduced on the previous one, thus showing again that science is of all things *the most unreliable*. It has floored itself, and proved that it is idle to hang any faith upon it. Yet, while it shows its incapacity to deal with demonstrations on the coatings of the human stomach, it presumes in the most *impudent* manner to pass judgment on the mysteries of spiritual phenomena, of which it can know much less than it does even of physical operations. Year after year it comes forward to deny the truths of spiritualism in the most *dictatorial* and *offensive* manner, while year after year spiritualism continues to advance with its proofs and to make captive the convictions of the human mind and heart. We may *reasonably* conclude, therefore, that science is a humbug, a pretender, a charlatan, not fit to be trusted with a judgment on any matter that involves such great interests as those involved in human beliefs."

My respect for Benjamin Franklin is so profound that I will make no comments on the above, nor seek to rob it of any of its weight. With this characteristic quotation (of spirital science,—not of Franklin) I close my collection of acquisitions to science.

Nearly a quarter of a century has elapsed since the first electric rap was struck which opened the line of communication between us and the spheres; and since that eventful hour, we are told by Professor Denton, "spirits make their presence known daily, hourly, to multitudes, not disdaining the poorest or the vilest." Plato has returned, and socially chatted in New York in English speech. Demosthenes again thrills the hearts of multitudes with his burning eloquence, through the inspired lips of Victoria C. Woodhull. Benjamin Franklin continues his interest in *scientific* subjects, and Shakspeare renews his acquaintance with the muse. Theodore Parker becomes an encyclopedic oracle, and Daniel Webster returns to correct mistakes in *his* dictionary! Lord Bacon discourses philosophy with Judge Edmonds, and the mirthful Calhoun indulges in antics under his table. And we have for results: in cosmology, the presence of spirit-architects for world-builders; in geology, a hollow globe, with an internal development of forms of life; in astronomy, races of salamanders living in the sun and major planets, and the discovery of the "spheres" "circling" the Milky Way; in geography, a vast continent lying around and *beyond* the north pole, exceeding in size the whole known surface of the earth, and the definite location of "Symmes's Hole;" in biology, the existence of "spiritual senses," which perceive what our outward senses had erroneously supposed to be the results of imagination as evidenced in delirium tremens; in astrology, the influence of the stars on character; in chemistry, the law of attraction between human bodies and precious metals.

In history, we have also valuable additions. Dr. Channing informs us that Jesus was an illegitimate child of Mary by Caiaphas, the high-priest; and the disclosures by St. Paul of his share in the betrayal of Jesus, and subsequent hypocritical assumption of belief, may be read at length in his work on "Jesus of Nazareth," as given through the organism of Alexander Smith. The influence of the planetary bodies on the formation of character, if a truth, might lead us to conjecture that the *lunar* orb had a prevailing influence in the horoscope of our spiritist friends.

Beyond these,—what? Savage and primitive in its forms of thought, ignorant and imbecile in its conception of uniformity in nature, arrogant and prejudiced in its investigations, partial and illogical in its collection of testimony and inferences therefrom, and contemptible and ridiculous in its vapid contributions to scientific knowledge, spiritism stands justly charged with being, in every sense of the term, unscientific.

CHAPTER II.

MODERN SPIRITISM UNPHILOSOPHICAL IN ITS TEACHINGS.

1. *In its materialistic spiritualism.*

"IN the early stages of human culture," says Dr. Alger, " when the natural sensibilities are intensely preponderant in power, and the critical judgment is in abeyance, whatever strongly moves the soul causes a poetical secretion on the part of the imagination. Thus, a rainbow is personified; a waterfall is supposed to be haunted by spiritual beings; a volcano with fiery crater is seen as a Cyclops with one flaming eye in the centre of his forehead. This law holds not only in relation to impressive objects or appearances in nature, but also in relation to occurrences, traditions, usages. In this way innumerable myths arise,—explanatory or amplifying thoughts secreted by the stimulated imagination, and then narrated as events."

Thus Fetichism slowly emerged as the natural result of man's necessities. Every forest, river, mountain, and glen had its own inward life; every tree, rock, and inanimate thing was endowed with a conscious personality. But, it has been often asserted, this tends to prove that religion and philosophy had their origin in ignorance of the natural causes of events. Not entirely so: through ignorance men offered their prayers or supplications to imaginary beings, but ignorance only caused the *misdirection* of their prayers; it was never the cause of their heart-felt need of prayer. This exists independently of fear and ignorance. Aspiration, the soul of all prayer, has its existence in the very constitution of mind, and in an ignorant age must necessarily have been manifested in other than an enlightened method; and from that remote epoch to our own time, man has never been able to shake off this feeling of dependence on the Unseen.

"As thought advanced," says Mill, "not only all physical agencies capable of ready generalization, as Night, Morning, Sleep, Death, together with the more obvious of the great emotional agencies, Beauty, Love, War, but by degrees also the ideal products of a higher abstraction, as Wisdom, Justice, and the like, were severally accounted the work and manifestation of as many special divinities." The conception of higher power could not exist in primitive minds, independent of the idea of form. By the very constitution of our minds, we cannot think of *things* at all, without calling into action the imaginative faculties which deal with mental pictures of material objects. To the primitive man these mighty spirits must necessarily be endowed with form, organs, and passions similar in nature to our own.

Long ages of steady advancement must have passed away before man could rise to a comprehension of the meaning of that grand statement—"God is Spirit!" And still how many there are who fail to even dimly discern the depth and beauty of that saying, and persist in regarding *form* as essential to *personality!* *Spirit* is illimitable, infinite; formless, yet not void; invisible, intangible, yet real. Goethe has said, and it is as true now as in prehistoric times, "Man is a true Narcissus; he delights to see his own image everywhere; and he spreads himself underneath the universe like the amalgam behind the glass."

On the part of our spiritist friends we find a similar

failure to comprehend the radical difference between spirit and matter. In fact, most of them fail to make any distinction whatever in essence, and recognize them as virtually one, spirit being etherealized matter, more highly rarefied than anything of which we are now cognizant; possessing less *density* than a physical *force*, permeating or passing through any form of gross matter, yet not affecting it physically.

We have it stated by "spirits," as reported by Judge Edmonds in his book on "Spiritualism," that "spirit-body or *spirit-matter* is intangible; and it is so sublimated that it is like electricity almost. We do not pass grossly through matter; but we *will*, and like a current of electricity we pervade matter. Our clothing is adapted to our conditions, and thus we are able to take with us what is on us." The illustrious Swedenborg has so far "progressed" since his advent in the spheres, as to have the following highly "spiritual" conceptions: "Now, spirits possess a material nature, and this nature, or form, in some is so gross that it is almost subject to laws as imperative as those on earth. *I mean as material laws.* Their material nature is under influences that require obedience, and though there is none of the physical suffering you have, yet there is as much *material* necessity and absolute want, in proportion to the grossness of their nature, as there possibly can be in your material world." "We eat and drink of the fruit of the countries where we reside." "The new spirit often finds it necessary to shelter its body from the sun or storm."

Swedenborg gives us the following pretty picture of the scenes which burst upon his *spiritual* vision on entering the *spiritual* world: "As soon as I reached the sixth sphere, I was conducted to my own home and left alone. I sank upon the grass, and listened to the exquisite singing of the birds. . . . I felt as though I was just born into a most beautiful world. I went to my bed, which was made of roses, and laid myself upon it, and in a dreamy state of happiness fell asleep."

" I dressed myself, and went into my garden. I saw all kinds of tempting fruit hanging upon the trees. . . . I took some of the fruit, and eat it. It was the first time I had tasted *spiritual* food!" "When I rose to the seventh sphere, I had but one guide, who carried a lamp." Probably to find the "opening" through which they were obliged to pass.* (" Supernal Theology.") Swedenborg's experience in the spirital world having been so extensive and varied, we are loath to part with so valuable a witness, and hence will quote again from him, as written through the mediumship of Dr. Dexter. He is again describing the beauties of the sixth sphere:

" The newness of everything impressed me with delight. The air was pure, and the whole heavens were clear and bright beyond all comparison. I saw no difference in the sky, except in its brightness and purity; and on looking abroad on the earth I could detect no difference in its appearance from our earth, except in the heavenly beauty and harmony in the arrangement of the landscape. The trees, the rocks and mountains, the flowers and birds, the gushing torrents and murmuring rivulets, the oceans and rivers, man, woman, and child, all passed before me." " We occupy earth,—tangible, positive earth,—as much as your earth ; but the *advanced* state of both *spirit* and *locality* renders it unnecessary for us to labor *much* to obtain food for the support of our

---

* " In rising to the spheres, there are openings through which we rise."
—*Supernal Theology*, vii.

bodies. Then, again, the earth brings forth spontaneously most of the food required for our bodies. Advanced spirits do not require as much food as those who are below them.—*Spiritualism,* sec. xv.

The " clear vision " of the seer is in accord with these angelic visitors. Andrew Jackson Davis reports as follows the result of his personal observations. " The Spirit Land ! What do you mean by these terms ? Something figurative, or something literal ? I mean a substantial world ; a sphere similar in constitution to this world, only in every conceivable respect *one degree* superior to the best planet in our solar system.

" What is the external appearance of the Spirit Land ?

" It appears like a beautiful morning ! The surface is diversified endlessly, with valleys, rivers, hills, mountains, and innumerable parks. These parks are particularly attractive. The ten thousand varieties of flowers lend a peculiar prismatic charm to the far-extending territories, and the soft divine ether in which the entire world is bathed surpasses all conception."—*Present Age and Inner Life,* p. 273.

The illustrious band of " spirits" who made the *Banner of Light* Free Circle their headquarters are no less explicit. Cardinal Cheverus is the respondent.

" *Ques.*—It is said that the spiritual body possesses all the organs of the physical body, and that there is nothing without use. If this be the case, of what use to the spirit are the teeth and stomach ? Do spirits eat food, masticating and digesting it, and passing it out of the system, in the spirit-world, as we do in this ? If not, of what use are the internal organs ?

"*Ans.*—The spirit-body possesses all the organs known to the natural body, and all the attributes, all the functions, known to the natural body, and more also ; for at each successive step in progress the spirit has need of new functions, new attributes, and the divine Providence provides for all it hath need of. Yes, the spirit hath a stomach, has teeth, and uses them. Spirits have need to eat, as you have. They do not subsist upon nothing. Here you are in the rudimental state of spirit-life, and here you eat. These spirits dwell in a more refined state, but there they eat also. Receive and give is the order of nature, divine and human. Therefore *all the processes* by which progress is carried on here, are known also and made use of in the spirit-world."—*B. of L.*, August 14, 1869.

On another occasion, when Theodore Parker was presiding, we have additional testimony. (As each "spirit" is only responsible for his own utterances, I desire to submit quotations from those whose utterances are deemed most authoritative, for, *of course*, the views of the *medium* are immaterial.)

"*Ques.*—Different answers have been given as to whether spirit-animals exist in the spirit-world. What information would you give with reference to that question?

"*Ans.*—There are spheres in the spirit-world where no animals exist; there are others where they do exist; but the sphere in which they are found most plentiful is that which is contiguous to your earth,—that which forms the inner sphere, or spirit-circle of your earth. These animals are a necessity to the inhabitants of the spheres in which they are found; they are not a necessity where they are not found.

"*Q.*—In more advanced spiritual spheres there is spiritual scenery; they have trees and plants, why not animals? We should consider the animal kingdom higher than the vegetable.

"*A.*—You say, in our 'more advanced spheres.' These

conditions exist in all spheres. We do not know why spirits are not found in all spheres, but we know they are not; no more than tropical flowers bloom in frigid zones. They are not a necessity there."—*B. of L.*, April 6, 1872.

Rabbi Löwenthal, through Mrs. Conant, describes a "spiritual home" as "dwellings surrounded by the beautiful in nature, perhaps by trees, water, shrubbery, flowers. All that goes to make up a beautiful rural home here generally *constitutes the beauty* of a spiritual home." —*B. of L.*, August 10, 1872. Father Fitz-James, another member of the "band," declares that all the various secret orders and fraternities existing among us "are perpetuated in the spirit-world, and all the various modes of protection against fraud, through outsiders, exist there as here."—*B. of L.*, June 8, 1872.

The "communications" from the spirit-world published recently under the title of "Strange Visitors," embracing articles on philosophy, science, government, and religion, from Irving, Willis, Thackeray, Richter, Humboldt, Sir David Brewster, and others, give us the same crass conception of spiritual existence. Margaret Fuller communicates an essay on "Literature in Spirit-Life." Professor Olmsted informs us of the "Locality of the Spirit-World;" Edward Everett contributes his more matured views on "Government;" Professor Bush discourses pleasantly on "Life and Marriage in Spirit-Life;" W. E. Burton informs us concerning "Acting in Spirit-Life;" and Charles E. Elliott tells us what he knows of "Painting in Spirit-Life." We have in this volume minute descriptions of "spiritual" architecture; and from the pen, if my memory serves me right, of N. P. Willis, we have a pen-and-ink sketch of a spiritual entertainment, where "spiritual" guests were served by "spiritual" waiters with "spiritual" food!

Andrew Jackson Davis has given the world some most searching criticisms and earnest rebukes of this grosser form of spiritism now so prevalent. His powerful protests against spasmodic and phenomenal spiritism entitle him to the highest respect as an independent thinker. No writer, however, has materialized spirit more completely than Mr. Davis. In his work, "*The Stellar Key*," we find the same error most grossly expressed:

"Until you come to perceive and comprehend these grand progressive truths, namely: that the solid world was once fluid; that fluid was once vapor; that vapor was once ether; that ether was once essence; that essence is the highest *material connecting link* for the operation of positive spiritual laws; that these natural inherent laws constitute a negative medium for the manifestation of invisible celestial positive force; that this force is the negative side of a yet more positive expression, called power; that this last potential demonstration is animated by interior intelligence and more positive energies, termed principles; that these immutable principles of the universe are external methods of positive and still more interior ideas; that ideas are the self-thinking, inter-intelligent, purely spiritual attributes and properties of the Divine Positive Mind." (P. 90.)

Are these the distinguishing characteristics of *spiritual* existence? The aspirations of the human mind are insatiable, ever ascending and approaching the attainment of higher and more spiritual development. Spiritual progression is more than the removal of the form from one material sphere into another; more than an entrance through an "opening" to another physical existence. The dying words of that highly-gifted and representative man, Goethe, "*More light*," are the soul's truest utterances, even though encased in a worn-out and enfeebled body, nearly ready to crumble into the dust. In the revelations made by the "spirits" we find no conception of true spirituality. Their arrangements of spheres, one rising above the other, with trap-door entrances, differ only in material aspect. The soul of man has higher and nobler aspirations than can be gratified with such crude conceptions.

The mind gives out its own phenomena without itself appearing, and originates in no previous phenomenal compound. It is not phenomenal, a state of some other things, but has its own successive states, while it perdures through them all. Nor is it ideal; for that presupposes a mind to construct the ideal, and the mind perdures through all its ideal constructions. All mental action is conditional to some object or end of action. There must be the agent acting, and the object or end of action, and the mind discriminates between them and assigns to each its own distinct identity. Its acts only appear in consciousness; and while its own successive states come and go, that still remains a something that produces them, which does not come and go. The mind lives under the act, and is a ground for it. Its agency is its own and originates its own causality. What mind is, remains an unsolved problem; and while we may have reason to conclude that it is not necessarily dependent upon the physical organization, but may survive it, we cannot picture to ourselves the conditions of its independent existence. To speak of mind, soul, and spirit as three distinct entities has no warrant in true spiritual philosophy. The desire of man to understand mental existence has necessarily led to physical expressions of it; living in a world of sense, we can apprehend only after its methods; but to assume that these expressions of mental existence are absolutely correct would lead any thoughtful mind to believe in materialism undisguised with pseudo-spiritualism.

Matter and mind should not be confounded; and their capacities cannot be judged from the same stand-point. Matter is but the outward form of existence. "The animal is built up, not by masonry from without, but by an organific power within, till he roams forth the effigy of the instinct that animates and rules him." But to attempt to bring this "organific power" within the compass of physiological laws as a physiological entity is more than we have any warrant for in philosophy.

As well talk of the form of thought, the weight of love, or the solidity of the affections, as to theorize on the attenuation of spirit. They are materialistic who assert the correlation of things so distinct, so opposed to each other, both in essence and function, through "the material connecting links" of essences, laws, and principles. To term such crassitude of thought and imbecile jargon spiritualism *par excellence* is emphatically unphilosophical.

2. *In its confusion of distinctions between physical and spiritual realms of being.*

The confusion of thought thus indicated pervades all spiritistic literature. Warren Chase, of the *Banner of Light*, asserts thought and love to be material substances. Dr. P. B. Randolph has treated of love in the same sense as a physician would of bile, as a material secretion. A lecturer advertises in the *Banner of Light* a course of lectures, the last of which has the following title, "Spiritualism and Materialism Uncontradictory," and adds, "As I am a *thorough spiritualist*, as well as a thorough infidel, I offer the last lecture as an alternative to those infidels who are also spiritualists."[*]

---

[*] November 9, 1872.

Spirital beings are described as of different degrees of grossness. "As they progress, they leave their grosser part from sphere to sphere;" but in each successive sphere we find cottages and husbandmen, palaces and privileged classes, those who serve and those who are waited upon. However "sublimated and etherealized" their bodies may be, still, as we have seen, they possess all the organs and functions of the physical body, and they can influence, control, or "obsess" mortals. In what manner are we controlled by these hybrid beings? Their material organism is too "sublimated and etherealized" to affect us physically, and their spiritual nature is too trammeled with bodily organization to have any influence on us spiritually. They pass through the most solid substances without leaving a trace of their presence, yet delight in physical manifestations. If they are *spiritual*, what influence can they wield over physical forces? how handle or direct electricity, magnetism, or psychic force? If they are *material*, as claimed, then their "influence" is a material influence, and no evidence of *spiritual* existence; for they are not from a distinct sphere of existence. If we are influenced by spiritual beings, it must be through our spiritual natures, and not through our physical nerves; the communication must come direct to the mind which, by the attainment of higher spirituality, has been drawn nearer to the spiritual world, to which our souls are ever attracted in their highest moments, nearer to the fount of all spiritual truth, closer in soul-relation with the higher realms of thought and existence. This is an inward, a subjective experience; not an outward, physical event induced by sitting at a table and harmonizing nerves and will.

God occupies an anomalous position in spirital theology. While assuming to be pantheistic, it bears no relation-

ship with the profound spiritualism of Spinoza, and looks pityingly on the "crude" views of Carlyle and Emerson. Swedenborg had some reputation while "in earth-life" of being versed in metaphysical philosophy, and the added years of experience and study in the highest spheres should lead us to expect his contributions to religious thought to be fraught with wisdom; yet, if we may believe Judge Edmonds, Swedenborg is capable of uttering the following unphilosophical expressions: "When the mind attempts to separate spirit from matter, it has no just conception of spirit. Therefore we cannot invest the Creator with form or personality. What sort of *person* would God be if the *form* depended upon the idea of man? The form would resemble that of man: as he is supposed to be the *image* of the Being who created him. There is no point from which an idea can be formed; and if, with all the various attributes with which the Creator is invested, there is but one point from which any resemblance could be traced, how utterly does the mind fail in carrying out this connection other than through the whole of God's manifestations of himself through his works! But the condition of matter necessary for such an *amalgamation* must be unknown to us as well as to you; for if the *identification of spirit with matter* were unfolded to your minds, the whole mystery of the Great First Cause would be understood."
—*Spiritualism*, sect. xxxi.

The above extract is not given to show that spirital theology is pantheistic, but to show the effect of spirital knowledge on the mind of Swedenborg,—that he, of all men, can return and commit so glaring an error as to confound form with personality, to speak of them as if they were identical or correlative in thought. We are told that God is a "Germ,"—the "Universal Germ."

"In short, God exists as a principle;" and it is added, "The soul of man is a part of God,"—a finite edition of an infinite "Germ;" too often an unprincipled portion of the omnipresent "principle." The following passage from Judge Edmonds's work on "Spiritualism" will most fully illustrate the confusion of thought existing among spiritists, and will need no comment:

"In short, God exists as a principle, . . . still resolving *itself* into direct and pertinent manifestations of the incomprehensible specialties of *his* nature. . . . God is the very spirit of life in everything; and *it* is eternally at work, sublimating and progressing every particle of *matter*, from the rudest form to *its ultimate end*, the immortal *spirit* of man!"

"The universal germ" is made more intelligible by being described as "pervading essence" with moral attributes!

In this same volume are communications from "my Lord Bacon" and "Daniel Webster," and heralded as "profound" contributions to modern thought.* "Daniel

---

* "Truly, if any man, who ever read ten lines of Bacon or one treatise of the thoughtful Swede, can believe that either of those men could have perpetrated, even in their school-boy days, such rhapsodical inanities as are there fathered upon their far-progressed spirits,—certainly credulity can no farther go, and never was known to go *so* far before.

"It cannot be said in this case, in order that the 'reader may find no difficulty in extricating his mind from doubts,' that it is 'an unwarrantable thing to look for instruction much superior to the mental development of the medium;' because, in the first place, these were reckoned rather uncommonly wise men while 'in the form,' and their spirits are now far progressed; and in the next place, the communications are kept clear of the *mind* of the medium, and only come through his arm. There remain, therefore, for all minds not precommitted to credulity, but two possible methods of solution of this difficulty,—the moral and intellectual absurdity involved in the asserted authorship of these communications: one is to suppose that these spirits were 'falsely personated,' and the other is to recur to the theory of Synesius, already referred to, and to suppose that the brain-dribble of the medium himself flowed down

Webster" is responsible for the following: "When we say light, we mean the *pure essence of God* that the *sun* reflects into your system. It is fraught with the life eternal; is the secret of your happiness, and the cause of your existence. . . . The partial obscuration of light at night is for the *resting of spirits.*" What terrible materialists our coal-miners and coal-consumers must be! for science has taught us to look upon coal as the tangible form of the solar rays " reflected into our system" millions of years ago, and they have calmly consumed countless tons of " pure essence" to satisfy material wants!

In their moral philosophy we find the same confusion of thought,—a failure to discriminate between the relative and the absolute. "Whatever is, is right," is regarded as an axiom, and, frequently held with the lowest and most depraved conceptions, is urged as an excuse for the most flagrant violations of the law of Right and Duty, which notwithstanding exists in humanity, and is ever manifesting itself when not followed.

> " Powers there are
> That touch each other to the quick, in modes
> Which the gross world no sense has to perceive;"

and to attempt the task by talking of Germs and Principles indifferently as *he* and *it*, or correlating Laws and Ideas by " the material connecting link" of Essences, is an unphilosophical confusion of

> " The seen and the unseen,
> The world of matter and the world of spirit."

---

through his arm upon the paper. Incredulous men will adopt, some one and some the other, of these solutions: for myself, I profess my most religious belief in the latter."—*Apocatastasis, or Progress Backwards* (Burlington, Vt., 1854), p. 170.

3. *In its claim of higher spirituality for rejuvenated polytheism.*

It has already been sufficiently shown that the only conception of the spiritual beings possessed by spiritists is that of "etherealized" material beings. God is a "Germ," indifferently termed *he* or *it*. Prayer is regarded as a vain attempt to change the purposes of an imaginary deity; destitute themselves of the faintest rudiments of spiritual perception, they *can* view it in no other light than that of offering advice or entreating material benefits. Spiritual truth is never attained through outward observances, and those who are truly spiritual never attempt to make these the means to that end. Spiritual truth is perceived from within, and true souls have lived in all ages who have been able to obtain glimpses of the higher life and its eternal realities. Not to allude to any whose names have become tiresome to spiritists rejoicing in the light of a New Dispensation, we will quote from Buddha, as one that obtained a few such glimpses even in his day, long before the tide of progression had reached the high-water mark indicated by modern spirital literature and "inspirational" lecturers.

The future state—*Nirvana*—is thus described by Buddha:

"The wind cannot be squeezed in the hand, nor can its color be told; yet the wind *is*. Even so Nirvana *is*, but its properties cannot be told."

"Nirvana, like space, is causeless, does not live nor die, and has no locality."

"Nirvana is not, except to the being who attains it."

"Nirvana is *real*, all else is phenomenal."

In that remote day this was regarded as very fair spiritual philosophy; but the waves of " progression" have borne us very far from it, to reach, in modern spiritism, "the spiritual philosophy of the nineteenth century," with its Demosthenes orators and Benjamin Franklin editors! Phenomenal spiritists are as deaf to the significance of these words of Buddha as they are to the spirit of the scientific thought of the age in which they live, move, and have at least a physical being. No "mysticism" will meet the requirements of their ardent souls. Their inner natures revolt from the "dry husks" of the past, and crave demonstrative evidence and a present intimate knowledge of the beautiful fields and fruitful orchards that lie on the other side of the "pearl-strand shore."

Although a distinguished itinerant orator has protested against the supposition that "spirits" are more than "men and women with their jackets off," still the greater body of spiritists do regard them in a far higher sense. They are supposed to inform us of approaching personal calamities; therefore, if true, we must accord them the power of reading the future by other means than by those afforded by the study of the past. Death is foreseen, and the exact moment of departure revealed to the interested individual: though death be the result of accident, the prescient mind of the "spirit" beholds it as plainly as we do the past. Their power over physical laws—a power, as we have seen, incapable of being reduced to a scientific knowledge of its extent or controlling laws—raises them higher than mere jacketless men and women, unless the chemistry of death effects some marvelous transformation in us; and this is not admitted by spiritists.

"*Congresses* of spirits," says J. M. Peebles (*alias* The Spiritual Pilgrim), "conceived the plan of laying the corner-stone of this late spiritual movement. . . . The propelling powers were spirits, angels, *heavenly hosts,*
c*

and God himself." "Congresses," "World-builders," neuter "Germs;" are not these the indications of polytheistic thought rather than of spiritual philosophy? In fact, the spiritists themselves glory in the points of resemblance between their system and ancient polytheism. "The Spiritual Pilgrim" wrote his "Seers of the Ages" to maintain this resemblance. A recent writer in the *Banner of Light* (of Nov. 9, 1872) makes the following declaration:

"Is phenomenal spiritualism a reality? In Hindostan, Egypt, and Greece, several thousand years ago, phenomenal spiritualism bore a striking resemblance to that of the present day. The statues and images representing what are termed the heathen gods and goddesses were in reality statues erected to the memory of their great men who had departed from the earth-sphere. They were made instrumental for obtaining spirit-manifestations, by the aid of mediums (priestesses), as at present. But we have no space to devote to this department, and hasten," etc., etc.

Willing to be made "instrumental" in imparting intelligence to our spiritist friends, a few instances of these ancient manifestations are here described for their benefit. Tacitus gives a description of the celebrated oracle at the fountain of Colophon, from which we extract the following: "There is not a woman here, as at Delphi, but a priest is elected from certain families, and mostly from Miletus, who is informed only of the name and number of those who come to consult the Oracle. He then retires into the cavern, and, drinking of the secret fountain, *though ignorant generally* of letters and poetry, he delivers responses, in verse, to whatever *mental questions* any one has in his mind."—*Annal.*, lib. ii. Here we observe several "striking resemblances," not only in the "manifestations," but in the character of the *medium* as well.

Let us continue our quotations. Herodotus relates the following: "Then was performed a great miracle. For Mus, as is related by the Thebans, having visited various oracles, came to the temple of Apollo Ptoi. There followed him three men publicly selected by the Thebans for the purpose of recording the responses which might be given. But on arriving at the temple they were astonished to hear the priestess answer in some foreign language, instead of speaking Greek, so that they had nothing to do. Whereupon Mus, taking from them their tablets, wrote down the responses of the Oracle; and, having made the record, he departed."—*Urania*. Considering that this was nearly twenty-five hundred years before the present "progressed" age, we must admit it was a very creditable "manifestation," and, were it not contrary to the idea of "progression," we might be led to regard it as more *demonstrative* than modern *Flashes of Light*.

As reincarnation is taught by modern "spirits," we may fancy that in the following extract from the geographer Strabo we have some information concerning the medium Home in his former state of existence: "Under Mount Soracte is the town of Feronia, which is also the name of the goddess of the place, who is held in great honor there. There is also a grove of Feronia, in which are performed sacred rites of a very wonderful kind. For those possessed by this dæmon walk with naked feet over burning coals and hot ashes, without suffering any injurious effects from the fire."—Lib. v.

"Spirit-forms" were also plainly discernible in that unprogressed age, and were made the subject of "scientific investigation." Porphyry gave evidence of possessing a critical spirit when he asked, "What is the indication of a god, or angel, or archangel, or demon, or a certain archon, or a soul, being present? For to speak *boastingly*, and to exhibit a *phantasm* of a certain quality, is common to gods and demons, and to *all* the more excellent genera." But the spirital philosophers were equal to the emergency; and the following scientific description and analysis of the manifestations was offered by Iamblichus,—a most competent authority and careful "investigator:"

"The phantasms, or luminous appearances, of the gods are uniform; those of demons are various; . . . those of souls are all various. And the phasmata indeed of the gods will be seen shining with a salutary light; those of archangels will be terrible; those of angels more mild; those of demons will be dreadful; those of heroes are milder than those of demons; those of archons produce astonishment; and those of souls are similar to the heroic phasmata. The phasmata of the gods are entirely immutable according to magnitude, form, and figure; those of archangels fall short in sameness; those of demons are at different times seen in a different form, and appear at one time great and at another time small, yet are still recognized to be the phasmata of demons; and those of souls imitate in no small degree the demoniacal mutations. . . . In the forms of the gods which are seen by the eyes, the most clear spectacles of truth are perceived; the images of demons are obscure; . . . and the images of souls appear to be *of a shadowy form*. Again, the fire of the gods appears to be entirely stable; that of archangels is tranquil; but that of angels is stably moved. The fire of demons is unstable; but that of heroes is, for the most part, rapidly moved. The fire of those archons that are of the first rank is tranquil, but of those that are of the last order is tumultuous; and the fire of souls is transmuted in a multitude of motions."

Here we have the testimony of one who has both used his eyes and mental faculties to some purpose, and has systematized the phenomena and orders of spirital beings, so that we may recognize each at once and determine the nature of the "influence." Here, also, we observe a more thorough acquaintance with the spirital world; for in ancient times communications from, and apparitions of, gods and demons, archangels and angels, heroes and archons, and, last in the scale, souls, were common events. Our modern "investigators" have only as yet recognized three classes, "spirits, angels, and heavenly hosts," and remain in entire ignorance of the superior powers known to the ancients, that manifested with their own particular "luminous appearance," as described above by Iamblichus. Let us continue our reference to this authority in things spirital, and observe the great benefit derived from understanding the characteristics of the spirital forms, and the danger of neglecting such a scientific classification of facts:

"That, however, which is the greatest thing is this, —that he who draws down a certain divinity sees a spirit descending and entering into some one, *recognizes* its magnitude and quality; and from this spectacle, the greatest truth and power of the god, and especially the order he possesses, as likewise about what particulars he is adapted to speak the truth, what the power is which he imparts, and what he is able to effect, *become known to the scientific.*"

Spirital science has yet much to accomplish to even regain what was known two thousand years ago, it would seem, when the above particulars could be determined at sight. Our "progression" must have been in a backward direction, as we may partly glean from the following, taken from the same scientific work, "On Mysteries:" " For when a certain error happens in the theurgic art, and not such autopic or self-visible images are seen as ought to occur, but others instead of these, then *inferior powers* assume the form of the more venerable orders, and *pretend to be those whose forms they assume;* and hence arrogant words are uttered by them, and such as exceed the authority they possess. . . . Much falsehood is derived from the perversion which it is *necessary* the priests should learn from the whole *order of the phasmata,* by the proper observation of which they are able to *confute* and *reject* the fictitious pretexts of those *inferior* powers, as by no means pertaining to true and good spirits."

Where now is the shade of Iamblichus? If Demosthenes can again thrill the hearts of men with his eloquence, and St. John hold sweet converse with "the Spiritual Pilgrim,"—if Joshua and Samuel have their latest word for sale at the *Banner of Light* counter, and Plato responds to Dr. Dresser in New York,—why can we not have the pleasure of hearing from Iamblichus again, and be kept from the danger of being misled by deceiving "inferior powers," from whom the very "elect" are not secure? Is it that this ancient sage is so thoroughly disgusted with the present management of the "theurgic art" that he will have none of it? or has he become reincarnated in human form, perhaps in the Jovian world? It is sad to think we have so deteriorated from the ancient standard, as is evidenced by the declaration of *our* seer that "it is an unwarrantable thing to look for perfect wisdom, or for instruction much above the mental development of the medium" !

Lucian informs us that the statue of Apollo in Syria, when neglected, would sweat and come forth into the room; and *once in his presence*, when borne by the priests, "he left them below upon the ground, while he himself was borne aloft and *alone in the* air." Iamblichus informs us that "to be borne along sublimely in the air" was one of the ordinary indications of inspiration in his day.

One more reference to ancient spiritism, and we will resume our study of its modern counterpart. Philostratus, in his life of Apollonius Tyanensis (book iii., c. 15, 17), relates this striking physical manifestation:

"'*I have seen*,' said Apollonius, 'the Brahmins of India dwelling on the earth and not on the earth, living fortified without fortifications, possessing nothing and yet everything.' This he spoke somewhat enigmatically; but Damis says they sleep upon the ground, but that the earth furnishes them with a grassy couch of whatever plants they desire. That he himself had seen them, *elevated two cubits* above the surface of the earth, *walk in the air!* not for the purpose of display [these were the *ancient* mediums, remember], which was quite foreign to the character of the men, but because whatever they did, elevated, in common with the sun, above the earth, would be more acceptable to the Deity. . . . Having bathed, they formed a choral *circle*, having Iarchus for their coryphæus, and, striking the earth with their divining-rods, *it rose up*,—no otherwise than does the sea under the power of the wind,—and caused them to *ascend into the air!*"

Did space permit, we should see all the phenomena recorded in ancient writers, and, unfortunately for the theory of "progression," far exceeding the records in our spirital papers. Mediums were then encircled with a luminous halo, and "spirit-forms" were each accompanied by a peculiar spirital spectrum, enabling us to immediately recognize their social standing and character for veracity. Voices were heard speaking from statues, musical manifestations abounded, and trumpets were then, as now, receptacles of spiritual truth. Suspension in the air, not only of mediums, but of statues and other inert bodies, was of common occurrence. All the various phases of the trance were well known, and spiritual beings manifested without the aid of a medium, producing spiritual writing and singing. Answering mental questions, and speaking in foreign tongues, were "tests" to many an anxious "investigator;" and, to carry out the "striking resemblances," many of the learned of that age regarded the revelations in the same light as their successors in this. Cicero said, "Some of them are the merest fiction, some, inconsiderate babble, never of any authority with a man of even moderate capacity." This conclusion bears a "striking resemblance" to that of Professor Huxley, who says, "But supposing the phenomena to be genuine, they do not interest me. If anybody would endow me with the faculty of listening to the chatter of old women and curates in the nearest cathedral town, I should decline the privilege, having better things to do. And if the folks in the spiritual world do not talk more wisely and sensibly than their friends report them to do, I put them in the same category.. The only good I can see in a demonstration of the truth of 'spiritualism' is to furnish an additional argument against suicide. Better live a crossing-sweeper than die and be made to twaddle by a medium hired at a guinea a *séance!*"

However deficient in a clear apprehension of the "theurgic art" our modern spiritists may be, some of them seem determined not to be outdone in the matter of marvelous relations. Take the following illustrations as a few out of many to be met with in spirital literature, and undoubtedly quite as authentic as any related of Apollonius. In the English edition of the biography of the Davenport brothers, by a Mr. Nichols, we may read the following " well-attested manifestation :"

" The strange event which took place is variously vouched for; but I have preferred to take the facts from the lips of Mr. Ira Davenport, the elder of the two brothers. He says he was walking one evening in the streets of Buffalo, with his brother William, this being the winter of 1853–4, and the boys in their twelfth and fourteenth years.

" Here Ira's recollection ceases. The next thing he knew was that he found himself and his brother in a snow-bank in a field, with no tracks near him, near his grandfather's house, at Mayville, Chautauqua County, New York, *sixty miles from* Buffalo. On waking up William, who had not returned to consciousness, they made their way to their grandfather's house, where they were received with surprise and their story heard with astonishment. Their father was immediately informed by telegraph of their safety and whereabouts; and he, good obstinate man, set himself to find out how they got to Mayville. On inquiry, he found that no railway-train could have taken them, after the hour they left home, more than a portion of the distance, and the conductors on the road knew the boys, and had not seen them. 'John' declared through the trumpet, after their return home, that he had transported them."

If it were not for the express declaration made by "John" that he had caused this wonderful flight, we should be tempted to believe that the "spirit" was no other than the lamented Peter Schlemihl, quondam possessor of the celebrated seven-league boots, concerning which we have read in more youthful days in an equally veracious history. In the American edition of the above work the foregoing narrative appears in a somewhat different form: being nearer home, and with, perhaps, the entirely unnecessary precaution of not "spreading it on too thick," we find that *one* of the brothers was transported across the Niagara River into a snow-bank on the Canada side. Reducing the number one-half, and the miles from sixty to two or three, would of course make the story seem less miraculous and more credible.

The writer has read descriptions of hundreds of manifestations, and witnessed scores, but for demonstrative purposes the following is yielded the palm, and commended to all inquiring minds anxious for spirital evidence. Nichols is again our authority:

"The room was not darkened, only obscured to a pleasant twilight. After several of the usual phenomena were exhibited, the two boys were raised from their chairs, carried across the room, and held up, with their *heads downwards*, before a window. 'We distinctly saw,' says an eye-witness, '*two gigantic hands attached to about three-fifths of a monstrous arm*, and those hands grasped the ankles of the two boys, and thus held the lads, *heels up and heads downwards*, before the window, now raising, now lowering them, till their heads bade fair to make acquaintance with the carpet on the floor!' This curious but assuredly not dignified exhibition was several times repeated, and was plainly seen by every person present. Among these persons was an eminent physician, Dr. Blanchard, then of Buffalo, now of Chicago, Illinois, who was sitting on a chair by the side of Elizabeth Davenport; and all present saw an immense arm, attached to no apparent body, growing as it were out of space, glide along near the floor till it reached Dr. Blanchard's chair, when the hand grasped the lower back-round of Elizabeth's chair, raised it from the floor with the child upon it, balanced it, and then raised it to the ceiling. The chair and the child remained in the air, without contact with any person or thing, for a space of time estimated to be a minute, and then descended gradually to the place it first occupied."

This demonstrative proof of immortality is deemed worthy of preservation in the American edition, where it may be seen with a full-page illustration of the brothers held in the arm, thus rendering assurance doubly sure. As this *two-handed arm* could not possibly have been one belonging to a jacketless man or woman, we may safely conjecture it must have been the personal property of one of Professor Lyon's "world-builders" who had graciously consented to aid the manifestations with his superior powers. We cannot, however, regard it as so much of a condescension, after all, for in thousands of "circles" the expenditure of a small amount of fractional currency may secure us the ineffable happiness of having our limbs pinched by Benjamin Franklin, in his moments of editorial relaxation, while George Washington tips the table!

Daniel Dunglas Home, whose aerial flights and spiritual elongations have made his name familiar with all, manifested his mediumistic powers at an early age, if we may credit his biography. We there find the following:

"On the 26th April, Old Style, or 8th May, according to our style, at seven in the evening, and as the snow was fast falling, our little boy was born in the townhouse, situate on the Gagarines Quay, in St. Petersburg, where we were still staying. A few hours after his birth, his mother, the nurse, and I heard for several hours the warbling of a bird, as if singing over him. Also, that night, and for two or three nights afterwards, a bright starlike light, which was clearly visible from the partial darkness of the room, in which there was only a night-lamp burning, appeared several times directly over its head, where it remained for some moments, and then slowly moved in the direction of the door, where it disappeared. This was also seen by each of us at the same time. The light was more condensed than those which have been so often seen in my presence upon previous and subsequent occasions: it was brighter and more distinctly globular."

The papers of Macon, Ga., during the month of October, 1872, gave long accounts of certain strange occurrences said to have taken place at a house not far from that city, on the Macon and Brunswick Railroad. Though "supernatural manifestations" have been more or less frequent for the past twenty years, it is only lately that the phenomena have become so violent. As this account is so recent, and so characteristic of modern polytheism, a report of it, not from a spiritistic source, may not be unwelcome. A reporter of the *Telegraph and Messenger* (Macon, Ga.) visited the scene of these phenomena, and from his account the extracts below are taken:

"Mr. Surrency's house is a two-story frame house, plastered and weather-boarded. Mr. Surrency, on returning home Thursday, the 10th instant [October, 1872], was astonished to observe the glass goblets begin to tumble off the slab, and the crockery to roll from the table and, falling on the floor, break into atoms. Books, brickbats, pieces of wood, smoothing-irons, biscuits, potatoes, tin pans, buckets, pitchers, and numerous other articles flew about the house promiscuously, without any visible cause. They seemed to spring up involuntarily, and often were never seen to move until they were shattered at the feet or against the wall.

"Late in the afternoon, while all the inmates of the house were at their supper, a noise was heard in an adjoining room. A gentleman was promptly at the door, the windows were all secured, and it was impossible for any one to escape without being observed. Presently a book fell in the passage, which only a few moments previous was certainly seen in the bookcase.

"On Monday the manifestations were again renewed in a more wonderful and frightful manner. While a company of ladies and gentlemen were seated in one of the rooms of the house, *a hog suddenly appeared* in the *middle* of the floor, and, without the slightest manifestation of fear, executed a few manœuvres and evolutions, when it quickly retreated to an adjoining room, where, in full view of the company, it suddenly vanished, like a ghostly apparition."

An apology may be deemed necessary for presenting the above; but such recitals as these compose the great bulk of "accredited manifestations," and are greedily swallowed by spiritists as "tests" of *spiritual* communion! If all that is absurd or contemptible in the subject were omitted, there *could* be no examination of spiritism. Let us again refer to the reporter's account, to see an accurate description of "investigation" after the spirital methods:

"An old *sea-captain*, who has been an eye-witness to the phenomena and demonstrations *incident to a sailor's life* and several voyages around the world, came to the place determined to solve the mystery. He watched with fixed attention for some time a smoothing-iron, which heretofore, by its supernatural exploits, seemed to be ring-master of the game. Becoming exhausted and *thirsty*, he *longed* for a bottle of the 'cratur,' which he understood was in the other room, when instantaneously the bottle fell on the floor at his side. *He partook of the liquor*, but the bottle disappeared as mysteriously as it came!" Truly a "new dispensation" is upon us if these tales find believing readers, even though it be one of a questionable sort.

The "spheres" are not always painted in the most gorgeous hues; for we find that many of their denizens are of an evil and repulsive character. Lying spirits return and are accredited with all the communications proving untrue. As sufficient space has been devoted to the power of the demi-gods and their modern Olympus, a few words on the abode of the "inferior powers," as old Iamblichus termed them, may not be out of place. Our modern polytheism has also its sombre abode, where dwell the "unprogressed" spirits, as they are termed in the "Whatever is, is right" theory; and this abode, we are informed, is the second sphere,—the one nearest to us; for we inhabit the first sphere, or "physical plane."

In all of the "spheres" we have seen material objects abounding, as on our "plane." Even in the highest "sphere," we are told by the spirital Swedenborg, "the land is subdivided into communities or neighborhoods, and in them the land is also again laid out in parcels *for each to till for the benefit of all.*" If the reward of spiritual growth consist in raising spiritual cabbages or etherealized potatoes for our neighbors, we may well wonder what is the penalty of living an "unprogressed" life on this "plane."

Dr. Dexter, or the "spirits" through him, informs us that "every soul that is out of keeping with divine order must remain in the license of a perverse will, forever vile, until restored by the regenerating influences of progression upward and onward forever." These "spirits" are necessarily in the lowest abodes,—their "unprogressed" condition rendering them more subject to the laws of gravity ; the weight of remorse causing them to gravitate to their appropriate *plane*, and this, as Judge Edmonds informs us, "embraces not only this earth, but many worlds." Here we find that the moral darkness resulting from being "out of keeping with divine order" is manifested in the black color of the bodies of all on this "plane." Consequently, we may regard a mulatto "spirit" as one already advanced on the highway of progression, and indeed "a man and a brother"! Small chance, however, has he for entering the "spiral paths" of progression, if we may credit Judge Edmonds's friends, as reported in "Spiritualism." Notwithstanding "the soul is a cosmopolite amid the eternity of worlds," yet it is led "by the force and direction of its affinities to select the associates with which it will daily mingle, and the neighborhood in which it will reside." Being controlled by "affinities" and "force of circumstances," these "spirits" lack, in the first place, the *disposition*, and, secondly, the "force of circumstances" presents some difficulty, for their "sphere" is an immense *plain*, as level as a Western prairie, with the exception of one high and rugged mountain in its centre, up whose sides winds the ascending path of progression. On this sterile plain farming leaves them but little time either for philosophical reflections on the state of their souls or ten-hour conventions for the relief of their bodies ; for "they toil for sustenance, and, as *their land is sandy, and no sunlight,* there must be great labor to enable the earth ['sphere'] to bring forth enough to sustain them." (Ibid., p. 222.)

This disposition for "higher life" is an essential prerequisite for climbing the central mountain, to obtain egress through the trap-door that opens to the sphere above. Evil passions and wicked propensities, or, in the new vernacular, an "unprogressed" condition, increase their specific gravity, and present a physical obstacle to mountain rambles; but a "sincere, dignified, elevated, soaring, self-sacrificing agony" of remorse and contrition has very much the same effect upon them as the introduction of hydrogen gas into a balloon, under the influence of which their spiral ascent grows easier each moment until the summit is reached, and with one elastic bound they spurn the sandy soil beneath them, and shoot upwards through the "opening" to "higher life," where they abide until a fresh inflation is possible, and then again to newer and brighter worlds, still upward! This is "progression."

Nor need we confine our attention to Judge Edmonds's work to find these crude polytheistic conceptions of the future life; for the illustrious band that control Mrs. Conant indorse many of these views. In the *Banner of Light*, of July 6, 1872, we find the "controlling spirit," Father Fitzjames, answering a question as to his first emotions on entering spirit-life. The reverend father gives a gloomy picture of his introduction to spirital scenes. He had yielded to temptation while "in the form," and became a drunkard. Let us listen to his experience: "When I entered the spirit-world, I found myself in a condition of unhappiness, and I was dissatisfied with my surroundings. . . . I wandered on for months. . . . I longed to soar away from my own darkness.

"*Ques.* (From the audience.)—I would inquire whether the darkness spoken of was merely mental, or was it objective darkness complementary to a mental condition? or whether it was anything similar to a lack of vision here?

"*Ans.*—It is a mental condition, and yet *it affects objective things.* I saw *beautiful* scenes, and met *beautiful* people, and they were all hideous to me. . . . The spiritual sun shone brightly, but I did not appreciate it any more than I did the sun of this life, which used to often shine brightly when I was drunk."

The following criticism on "life in the spheres," from some unknown pen, is so pertinent that I gladly quote it here:

"To illustrate the extreme sublimation to which constant attrition and metamorphosis have at length drawn out the physical man (in the seventh sphere), we are exultingly told that many of the higher spirits have no need to eat oftener than once a week! Taking that as the basis of a calculation, we may easily discover the precise ratio of their fineness to the texture of our own mortality. Once a week to three times a day! That would make one bricklayer of Gotham equal, in a fair fight, to about *twenty-one* spherical farmers of the very highest capacity!"

Need more be said to show the parallel existing between ancient polytheism and modern spiritism,—not only similar in philosophy and phenomena, but accounting for errors by similar methods? Read the following extracts from the ancient believers, and see how closely they tally with the reasoning of our modern pagans:

"There are some who suppose that there is a certain obedient genus of demons, which is naturally fraudulent, omniform, and various, and which assumes the appearance of gods, and good demons, and the *souls of the* deceased, and that through these everything which appears to be either good or evil is effected." (Porphyry to the Egyptian Anebo.)

In another place he says,—

"By the contrary kind of demons all prestigious effects are produced. They constantly cause apparitions and spectral appearances, skillful by deceptions which excite amazement to impose upon men. *It is their very nature to lie;* because they wish to be considered gods." (Porphyry apud Eusebium.)

"Evil spirits, after a fantastic and fallacious method, *simulate* the presence of gods and good demons (spirits), and therefore command their worshipers to be just, in order that they themselves may seem to be good like the gods. Since, however, they are by nature evil, they willingly induce evil when invoked to do so, and prompt us to evil. These are they who in the delivery of oracles [messages] lie and deceive." (Iamblichus.)

The following, we might almost venture to say, must have been "inspirational:"

"But an intellectual perception, above all things, separates whatever is contrary to the true purity of the phantastic spirit; for it attenuates this spirit in an occult and ineffable manner, and extends it to divinity. And when it becomes adapted to this exalted energy, it draws, by a certain affinity of nature, *a divine spirit* into conjunction with the soul: as, on the contrary, when it is so contracted and diminished by condensation that it cannot fill the ventricles of the brain, which are the seats assigned to it by providence, then, nature not enduring a vacuum, *an evil spirit is insinuated* in the place of one divine." (Synesius.)

"These impure spirits . . . *gravitate downwards*, and seduce from the true God towards matter, render life turbid, and sleep unquiet: *gliding secretly into the bodies of men,* they simulate diseases, terrify the mind and distort the limbs." (Minutius Felix.)

"The regions of the air are filled with spirits, who are

demons and heroes; that from them come all kinds of divination, omens, etc.; that all kinds of divination are to be held in honor." (Pythagoras.)

Compare the last quotation with the following inspirational gem from the " spirit" Theodore Parker:

"*Ques.*—How does a fine normal speaker, such as Henry Ward Beecher, differ from a medium under what we term inspirational control?

"*Ans.*—The difference is simply in degree; for all fine speakers are inspirational speakers. They cannot be fine speakers unless they are open to the truths that exist in life; and therefore they are inspirational *mediums.*" *B. of L.*, Nov. 16, 1872.

"O Achilles, the many assert that you are dead, but I do not coincide with that opinion, neither does Pythagoras my master. If we are right, show us your shadow. For allow me to say that my eyes might be of much service to you, could you use them as witnesses of your being alive." (Apollonius Tyanensis.)

"* * * holding conversation with the shades *and* spirits of the deceased." (Pliny.)

In the editorial columns of the *Banner of Light* (of Nov. 16, 1872) is an allusion to a suicide-cell in a prison, in which several persons have hanged themselves. There is nothing so very remarkable about this in itself, for similar narratives may be met with in almost every work on mental philosophy; but spiritual science has solved the mystery. A young girl who had attempted suicide in this cell was restored to life, and said that "a little white woman" had appeared to her in the night, and " persuaded her" to hang herself. "*To test the matter*, a stranger—a man—who had applied for a night's lodging was put into the cell, with a full knowledge of its character. At a certain hour he was visited by the same little white woman, who tried to persuade him to do the deed she had led others to do before him. He was in due time relieved of his painful suspense, and told his story, though he was not previously apprised of the visit of the little woman. It appears that some time ago such a woman did hang herself in that cell, and she revisits it regularly to gratify her propensity as often as the temperament or condition of the occupant allows her."

In this case the cell is the *medium*, it will be observed, for the exercise of her evil "propensity." I shall make no comment on this, but, together with the analogous quotations from more ancient writers, lay them before the reader to show the identity of thought between the two classes of spiritists.

If *spirituality*, or its modern equivalent, "sublimation," is acquired only as we recede from the earth to higher "spheres," we may fairly question whether the acquaintance is desirable of those in the "spheres" nearest the earth, whether the black and tawny "spirits" that have not as yet progressed by the exhilarating agony of remorse out of the "sphere" adjacent to us are, after all, the safest guides to enlighten us on *spiritual* duties! The spiritist will accept the quotations above as confirmatory of the truth of his position, but the thoughtful reader will hesitate to accredit a theory on such questionable credentials.

Throughout the whole jargon of words constituting the so-called "spiritual philosophy of the nineteenth century," we find in the "accredited manifestations" and descriptions of the "spheres" only a weak and contemptible rejuvenation of the polytheism of ruder ages.

4. *In its fallacious mental philosophy.*

The genuine spiritist recognizes no such thing as *genius*. "Spirit-power" is claimed for every act done, word spoken, or emotion felt. Every invention with which the world has been blessed is the result of ideas impressed on the mind by unseen beings. Every poet, from Shakspeare and Burns down to the trance-medium, is only a vehicle for *inspiration* from "the invisibles." All our orators, from the most eloquent statesman, whose burning words have kindled into a flame the souls of a whole nation, even to the itinerant spiritist lecturer that charms the gaping crowd, are but puppets in the hands of those who hold the wires on the unseen side of life. Our very dreams are revelations of the higher life, and have been carefully studied and their significance tabulated by a distinguished spiritist, in a "Book of Dreams," and advertised in spirital papers.

Even those who are entirely unaware of the presence of "intellectual guides" are as certainly under their influence as any of the well-known *media*. The editor of the principal journal of this modern "spiritual philosophy" (assisted by the jacketless Franklin) recently assured me that, by long experience in inspired writings, he could instantly detect the extent of inspirational control in any article sent to him for publication, and he had frequently noticed in my contributions convincing evidence of a high degree of "inspirational control." Hence the reader may view these pages as the work of some paradoxical "spirit" that has not as yet progressed to the possession of a ten-acre lot in the higher "spheres," but is awaiting, on the sandy plain of the lower region, the necessary inflation for an upward course.

J. M. Peebles, "the Spiritual Pilgrim," for many years one of the editorial corps of the *Banner of Light*, asserts, in his "Seers of the Ages," that every act performed by the "psychologist" upon his subjects can only be explained by being viewed as the influence of the denizens of the other world. The well-known phenomena of impressions transmitted from one mind to another, loosely classed together under the term *clairvoyance*, are universally regarded by spiritists as test-manifestations, and *media* relate that while under the control of the "influence" using their organism for the time being, their own spirit is traveling in other places, often in Europe, or other far-distant lands.

Disembodied spirits have been accredited with inspiring the mind of Edgar A. Poe when he was with us, but the brighter light of this newer philosophy shows us that the vinous stimulants were only the agencies employed for harmonizing his mind into the condition of "passive receptivity" necessary for catching the "music of the spheres." Thus we become mere "spouts," to use A. J. Davis's appropriate word, through which the inspiration of others is poured. If indeed Poe was incapable of any original mental power, but was a mere automatic distributer of ideas injected into his mind, we might well wonder how he could now, in his jacketless condition, be able to do nearly, if not quite, as well through the physical organisms of others, as admirers of his recent poetical communications believe.

The laws of mind are only to be studied and understood in the light of mediumship. Genius is a plant indigenous to the higher latitudes of the "spheres," whither *all* forms of life are tending, for all animate and inanimate forms have their indwelling spiritual entity,—a "sublimated" body which still lives on in the other life. Immortality is not more peculiar to man than to the pig or the tree.

> "Pig, bullock, goose, must have their goblins too,
>   Else ours would have to go without their dinners:
> If that starvation doctrine were but true,
>   How hard the fate of gormandizing sinners!"

Spiritism, though claiming to be as yet but a child in years, is really an old friend of extremely antiquated appearance, being as old as human ignorance. When it is critically examined, we discern it to be strutting in borrowed clothing and betraying, by its confusion of thought, more affiliation with the rude polytheistic conceptions of ancient Greece, Rome, and Persia than with the analytic mental philosophy of our day, and hence, notwithstanding its high pretensions, unphilosophical and gross in its teachings.

CHAPTER III.

MODERN SPIRITISM UNNATURAL IN ITS EFFECTS.

1. *In its effect on mental health, by destroying self-reliance.*

TRUE mental health can only consist in the untrammeled use of our intellectual faculties through their normal development. The old reply of the plowman to the dyspeptic inquirer, that he " had no system," was an indication of physical health. The healthy man has no knowledge of the operations performed by his secretory organs. In health they perform their work silently and naturally, and only disease brings them into prominence in our consciousness; they have then assumed an *unnatural* character, and we are forcibly reminded of their existence. Even so in mental and spiritual health; the organs of the mind must work with a natural spontaneity, neither forced nor starved.

Whatever assumes to give us a royal road to knowledge in any direction other than that worked out by our own faculties, or pretends to reveal to us the mysteries of time, is unnatural, and would produce an unhealthy state of mental growth. Man must hew out his own knowledge, rather than obtain it by gift, if he would not stagnate in imbecility. The *use* of organs must be under the direction of our consciousness: if we neglect the use or remit it to others, the result is the same. By a process of natural selection, the *disuse of organs* renders them practically worthless. As the Hindu devotee that stands upon one foot for years sees the other limb shrink and wither from disuse, so the surrender of our minds for the thoughts of others, while we remain unconscious of such use, can never prove otherwise than injurious to mental health.

Thought kindles thought. As the light applied to the slow-match sends activity into the heart of the rock, so does an idea once fully possessed awaken a train of ideas, until the whole shell, in which custom so often encases the mind, shakes and crumbles away before its active powers.

If our ideas are obtained by impressions from without through mechanical means, mental activity can never ensue. The organs of man are the *outlets* of an indwelling controlling force, not the *inlets* of knowledge by external control; man is an intelligence served by organs, not a mere instrument to be played upon. Man has a nobler mission than serving as a spiritual wateringpot in the hands of any hypothetical "influence," either of the earth earthy, or of the "spheres" sublimated!

The grand prerequisite for mental independence, the condition of health, is to have a *soul* within us, an animating, invigorating, inspiring soul,—not an etherealized phantasm of the physical man, who is to continue his etherealization through a sevenfold existence hereafter, unless sooner reincarnated, but a soul that can recognize divine order here, and by and through its own faculties put itself in keeping with *it;* something in *us* that will stir up all our slumbering powers into new activities under the dominating rule of a *purpose;* without which we may as well be automatic implements in the hands of others, mere voluble dischargers of second-hand thought, with even the wadding furnished; *for without soul— *purpose*—all powers are useless.

What is it to us to know that "the first sphere is the natural, the second the spiritual, the third the celestial, the fourth the supernatural, the fifth the super-spiritual, the sixth the super-celestial, the seventh the Infinite Vortex of Love and Wisdom"? No! nature's divine revelations teach us not of the names of *conditions* of being held in store by her, but to so live and develop our own transcendent powers as to insensibly pass into those higher conditions.

> " To know that which before us lies
> Is the prime wisdom; what is more is fume,
> Or emptiness, or fond impertinence,
> And renders us in that which most concerns us
> Unpracticed, unprepared."

Words are but the garments of thought. Terminology should never take the place of the animating idea. Thought, which necessarily clothes itself in action, is needed to make the truly self-reliant man. Soul *once* attained, all is attainable; for where purpose exists, action will result, and so far as the actions are the result of spontaneity, is mental health indicated.

Many of our spiritist friends seem to regard mental action as a mechanical influx, instead of a spontaneous outgrowth; no inner fire burns on the hearth to warm the whole man into a glow of healthy activity, rousing a passive will into a sovereign principle, but we are offered the cold reflection of distant star-beams, which, however deep they may pierce, can excite no molecular motion. The man of purpose cannot remain the *passive* shuttle-cock of contending forces, " compelled to act as he is acted upon,"* but resolutely seizes the refractory circumstances, places a bit in their mouths, and renders them subservient to his will. Intensely realizing the duties of the present, he has

---

* "The Great Harmonia," vol. ii. p. 225.

neither time nor inclination to spare in profitless inquiries concerning the vocations and avocations of the departed.

"Life is real, life is earnest;"

and a healthful, natural condition of the mental faculties rejects all external developing processes of the mechanical sort, as savoring of the quack. Manly self-reliance, therefore, is not attainable by placing ourselves under the control of others, whether in a physical or sublimated body; not in the school of mediumship do we learn better to battle the waves of life as they surge around and over us. Only in the development of *our own* mental powers, under the master-hand of soul, recognizing in life a purpose, and unconsciously outworking every thought into action, can we ever arrive at a healthful activity of the mind.

Inspiration, of the mechanical kind, declares man to be "a gland or minute organ" in the "great Body of the Divine Mind,"* a species of Æolian harp to be played upon; but another inspiration, not of the baser sort, moved the mind of Matthew Arnold when he wrote these lines:

"From David's lips this word did roll,
'Tis true and living yet:
No man can save his brother's soul,
Nor pay his brother's debt.

"*Alone, self-poised*, henceforward man
Must labor, must resign
His all too human creeds, and scan
Simply the way divine."

Is the "spiritual philosophy of the nineteenth century" to become a mechanical one, confuting materialism and soulless sadduceeisms by converting the mind into a mechanical trough, with the sole faculty of "pas-

---

* "Nature's Divine Revelations," p. 263.

sive receptivity"? Those sparks from the inner hearth where the soul sits enshrined, and known in mortal speech as ideas, talent, genius, are not to be reduced to a phantasm or worshiped as *super*-human, but reverently regarded as dim signs of almost infinite possibilities. Inspiration does dwell in the innermost recesses of the soul, and is often manifested, notably so in these words of Carlyle, which many might read with profit:

" 'Man of Genius:' O Mæcenas Twiddledee, hast thou any notion of what a man of genius is? Genius is 'the inspired gift of God.' It is the clearer presence of God Most High in a man. Dim, potential in all men; in this man it has become clear, actual. So says John Milton, who ought to be a judge; so answer him the voices, the Voices of all Ages and all Worlds. Wouldst thou commune with such a one? *Be* his real peer, then: does that lie in thee? Know thyself and thy real and thy apparent place, and know him and his real and apparent place, and act in some noble conformity with all that. What! The star-fire of the Empyrean shall eclipse itself, and illuminate magic-lanterns to amuse grown children? He, the god-inspired, is to twang harps for thee, and blow through scrannel-pipes, to soothe thy sated soul with visions of new, still wider Eldorados, Houri paradises, richer lands of Cockaigne? Brother, this is not he; this is a counterfeit; this twangling, jangling, vain, acrid, scrannel-piping man. Thou dost well to say with sick Saul, 'It is naught—such harping!' and, in sudden rage, to grasp thy spear and try if thou canst pin such a one to the wall. King Saul was mistaken in his man, but thou art right in thine. It is the due of such a one: nail him to the wall, and leave him there. So ought copper shillings to be nailed on counters, copper geniuses on walls, and left there for a sign!"

2. *In its effect on spiritual health by fostering superstition.*

What is superstition? Who shall decide for us what is superstitious? Webster, it is true, defines superstition as excessive exactness or rigor in religion, and as belief in omens and prognostics. As to the first, it may be questioned whether excessive exactness or rigor can exist in religion itself, and we may conclude that the "excess" is a sign of no religion, a mere sham substitute for religion. If, however, is meant a rigor in what is called religion by those in whom we think we discover the symptoms of excess, we should then conclude that exactness must never overstep a certain line which still remains indefinite. How far shall we be exact to our conceptions of truth and duty without overstepping the boundary-line between the rational and the irrational, and entering the domain of superstition? I think I am not a superstitious man, and I discover that my neighbor has the same good opinion of his own rationality. So we are again brought to our starting-point: What *is* superstition?

John Wetherbee, in a thoughtful article published some time since in *The Index*, though professing not to be able to answer the question, still felt certain that there was "no body of people, in Christendom or out of it, so free from superstition as the modern 'spiritualists.'" If all spiritists were as sensible as Mr. Wetherbee, these pages would be unnecessary; yet even he did define it, in his estimation, as "the dry-rot of the Christian church," a definition aptly illustrating our proneness to discover the mote often existing in our neighbor's eye, and recalling to mind a remark attributed to Josh Billings, that the best place to have a boil was somewhere on your neighbor's body!

If we say belief in omens and prognostics—that physical signs or events in the natural world are material evidence of spiritual facts—does it remain clear that Mr. Wetherbee's friends are of all bodies the most free from this charge? Mr. Wetherbee declares of his belief that "its most accented expression is that everything is natural and nothing supernatural. The moment a man is a believer, he can be superstitious only so far as he is inconsistent. A man may be credulous; he may be shallow; he may be ignorant: these are human attributes, and may appear in human beings who are spiritualists. But the subject tends to correct all such weaknesses."

Is this indeed true? Does an "instantaneous conversion" occur "the moment a man is a believer"? or is this assertion but what any sectary announces of his own pet theory of the universe? Does an earnest, entire belief in the presence of our departed friends, and the possibility of conversing with them on any subject, tend to render us more self-reliant and less credulous? Does the possibility of consulting a trusted friend removed to a higher plane with a broader scope of vision, and the adoption of his advice, tend to eliminate shallowness? If belief in such intercourse *tends to correct* ignorance, is the extent of the correction in any proportion to the intensity of the belief? Are they who believe least, or they who believe most, the most intelligent in the ranks of spiritism?

Mr. Wetherbee's articles invariably bear evidence of their author's possessing good common sense; whether his faith or his skepticism is the greater always appears to me a matter of doubt, but not which is more in harmony with his common sense.

Let us take a closer view of the field, and by comparison see if we can place our hand on any one belief and say, This is indeed superstitious. I read that a Tartar shaman lies in a lethargic slumber while his soul journeys in other lands, or visits the realms of the departed. In former years I was accustomed to look on this as superstitious, but the light of the New Dispensation has made the phenomenon as common among us as with the Tartars; for I read in the *Banner of Light* (of August 31, 1872) a communication from Ohio, setting forth the wonderful manifestations performed by "invisibles" in that State, where soul-communion is attained through the humble instrumentality of a tin trumpet. The souls of all present having been harmonized by an influx of spirituality, radiating from the aforesaid trumpet of tin (is tin preferable to other metals as a conductor of spiritual influence to our spiritual natures? A query for spirital science), the writer adds, "Miss Annie M——, a member of the circle, passed into a clairvoyant state, and remained for a time entirely under the control of departed spirits, who spoke to us through her, while her spirit, in the mean time, wandered with our spirit-friends amid the beauties of the brighter world, a recollection of which she always retains, and relates to us as soon as her spirit takes charge of her earthly form." Shall we say the Tartar or the degraded Bushman is irrational and superstitious for believing in Asia or Africa what in America is not only rational, but *the* rational method of correcting credulity, shallowness, and ignorance?

I have been accustomed to see superstition in the belief of savage tribes in spectral appearances; to regard apparitions as subjective only in origin; to believe that in hallucination

"The soul—
Wrapt in strange visions of the unreal—
Paints the illusive form."

But the familiarity of our own friends with ghostly

acquaintances must lead us to revise our judgment of Karens or Caribs, or to extend the borders of superstition to include many in our midst. When I read in the *Banner of Light* (of February 11, 1871) a detailed account of the return of a "spirit," who manifests his presence by purloining corn from a reverend gentleman's corn-crib, opening windows, and scattering culinary furniture, I am forcibly reminded of the agreement between the savage and the *Banner* writer in their interpretation of phenomena, and have no doubt they would still further agree that superstition is a deadly weed and should be eradicated whenever found on our neighbor's ground.

To believe that our friends are ever with us, and anxious to impart counsel and assistance in our many perplexities, would inevitably lead the mind to listen to their monitions, coming as we would believe from a being of a higher condition, and removed from the influence of the petty things which contract our vision here; in inverse proportion to our belief in the reality of their presence and communications would be our inclination to calmly weigh their words in our mind. To *test*, to weigh in the scales of reason, is to doubt, to be uncertain whether the phenomenon does proceed from the source claimed; and our spiritist friends claim to have *knowledge*, not faith. Mediums often boast of the numbers that come to them to consult their friends in higher life regarding their business speculations, and claim that thousands never make any venture unless it has received indorsement from these friends. And this claim is consistent with the spirital theory; for the whole tenor of the "philosophy" is to show that "spirits" can not only impart information, but that they possess better means of forecasting the future than mortals still confined in the "cramping influence of material environments."

A story was recently current of a young lady in Maine having been married to the sublimated form of her deceased lover. Was this act any evidence of superstition? If he was with her, visible in bodily form to *her* eyes, and she could converse with him and hear the words that passed his spiritual lips, why not become in fact, what she was in intention, his wife? "Material" minds may indeed regard her action as superstition, but not so the spiritist. Admitting the premises, no such conclusion could possibly follow. He would regard her as having attained to a clear conception of *real* things, a knowledge of spiritual truth,—confessedly the highest development, —and the conversation of her sublimated husband would necessarily tend to broaden her field of vision, and eliminate credulity, shallowness, and ignorance.

Leaving the spiritist firm in his "knowledge," we will not need to seek further for an answer to the question, " What is superstition?" for if the ground on which superstition is produced be once regarded as true knowledge, and assiduously cultivated, we need not marvel that spiritist writers confess their inability to define superstition.

In discussing the effects of spiritism on the mind, I would not be supposed to assert that all spiritists are superstitious. I do not regard Mr. Wetherbee as a superstitious man; not, however, because his belief has eradicated superstition but for the reason that he has not accepted all the *logical conclusions* of the spirital theory.

I have in several places criticised some of the written expressions of A. J. Davis as materialistic and gross, yet Mr. Davis has ably protested against some of the popular views current among spiritists. As an act of justice to him, I here quote from one of his recent works —" The Fountain"—his views on "popular errors."

Whether he is strictly logical in affirming the "philosophy," and denouncing as errors what others regard as essential elements of it, is another question, on which we should undoubtedly differ.

"Among the errors and hurtful superstitions which have sprung up in modern fields—in fields where we fondly hoped the immortal flowers of reason alone would grow and forever bloom—I will in this place mention only nine, as follows:

"1. That departed spirits, both good and evil, continually float and drive about in the earth's physical atmosphere.

"2. That evil-disposed characters, having died in their active sins, linger around men and women both day and night, in order to gratify their unsatisfied passions and prevailing propensities.

"3. That all known mental disturbances, such as insanity, murder, suicide, licentiousness, arson, theft, and various evil impulses and deeds, are caused by the direct action of the will of false and malignant spirits.

"4. That certain passionate spirits, opposed to purity and truth and goodness, are busy breaking up the tender ties of families, and take delight in separating persons living happily in the marriage relation.

"5. That spirits are at all times subject to summons, and can be 'called up' or made to 'appear' in circles; and that the 'mediums' have no private rights or powers of will which the spirits are bound to respect.

"6. That spirits are both substantial and immaterial; that they traverse the empire of solids, and bolt through solid substances, without respecting any of the laws of solids and substances; and that they can perform anything they like, to astonish the investigator.

"7. That every human being is a medium in one form

or another, and to some extent; and that all persons, unconsciously to themselves, are acting out the feelings, the will, and the mind of spirits.

"8. That spiritual intercourse is perpetual; that it is everywhere operative; and that, being at last established, it cannot be again suspended.

"9. That the reading of books, and reflection, as a means of obtaining truth, are no longer necessary to believers; that the guardian band of spirits will impart to the faithful everything worth knowing; and that, for anything further, one need only wait upon the promptings of intuition; and that, in any event, 'whatever is is right.'

"These errors, these superstitions, and these dogmas, like all other human developments, contain rich intimations and germs of truth. These theories have taken deep root among a large class of avowed spiritualists. And the legitimate effects, it will be remembered, are visible in the disintegrations and decompositions of character; in mutual disrespect and recriminations; in the disorganization of all our public efforts and the abandonment of our beneficent enterprises; in the irreverence manifested towards even the great central principles around which all persons and facts must bow and cling; and, lastly, in the gradual suspension of the delightful intercourse itself, by which the glory and unspeakable opportunities of immortality have been brought to life.

"After twenty-five years of constant investigation into the many and various phases of this subject, and with almost daily realizations of somewhat of the infinite goodness embosomed in these high privileges, I can most solemnly affirm, and I do now make the declaration, that the nine propositions contained in the indictment are mostly errors and hurtful theories, injurious in their effect upon the individual judgment, and still more injurious when made the foundation of faith and practice. They belong to the age of broom-riding witches, to the shallow doctrines of personal devils and sorcery, and the fiction age of astrology and the small gods of superstition. They will not bear analysis by the philosophical method of detecting the presence and value of truth. They will not stand a test by the supreme infallible authorities,—*Nature, Reason, Intuition.*"

3. *In its effect on physical health by developing abnormal faculties.*

That the healthful know not of their health, but only the sick, we have seen to hold true in a far wider sense than its physical one. Health is a state of unconscious activity of all normal faculties. All faculties are normal or abnormal according to the *use* made of them. Webster defines *abnormal* as "irregular, contrary to rule," and hence any faculty used irregularly, and not according to the established methods of nature, is abnormal and unnatural.

The mental and physical are too intimately correlated for one not to be affected by whatever tends to weaken the other. Anything which tends to sap or destroy the natural activity of the organs through which man holds converse with objective nature tends to lower the standard of health, for the abnormal use of any faculty being "irregular" *must* so far weaken it for normal service. To attain physical manhood, we must ourselves have control of the reins, and not be held or swayed from without.

"Man is an intelligence served by organs," and these organs may have a stinted or an excessive development; but in either case they should remain our own. If we grant the assumption of the spiritist, that even now

> "The unseen
> Shore faint resounds, and all the mystic air
> Breathes forth the names of parent, brother, wife,"

and that we may become *media* for their use in conversing with those remaining on the shores of time, we should still regard the method adopted as one detrimental to physical perfection, and unnatural.

Our organs of speech will but give what there is in us to say, whether wise or otherwise. If we have the thought, an inspiring idea, it will soon enough clothe itself in articulate words and go on its way, doing its mission wheresoever it may find lodgment. Ideas are never isolated. "One-idea men" are illusive monstrosities, existing nowhere in nature, for ideas are creative; they are active, agitating, fruitful, filling the mind with light and eventuating in healthful action.

If the *thought* be not there, but only a barren waste, destitute alike of beautiful verdure and refreshing springs ever overwelling, and "passively" content with reflecting the rays falling upon it, instead of absorbing and outworking them, the natural end and purpose of existence is wanting, and action of a manly sort can never ensue. Man is not a machine whose motive power may be estimated in terms of beef or grain; he is more than the sum of his senses, and must be *master* of his faculties to even develop physical manhood. The child that is always waited upon, whose every wish is gratified, that finds no occasion for inquiry or thought, remains a child; he never reaches manhood, whatever may be his longitudinal standard. If we are to become mere auxiliaries to tin trumpets for the transmission of the wisdom of the "spheres," there must be an arrest of normal growth, and manhood lies not in us, but far removed from us.

Nature, with all her reticence as regards herself, is prodigal in her gifts, and has bountifully supplied us with faculties for perceiving truth and beauty, if we would but use them, and methods for giving expression to them infinitely better than we can find through any other channel never adapted to the purpose; methods far more inspiring than "passive receptivity" to every Tom, Joe, or Harry that may desire to give vent to spherical idiocies or sentimental drivelings.

If we could thus be used by entirely unknown persons, subject to questionable—ay, often unquestionable—"influxes," and our divine faculty of speech be made a trumpet of uncertain tone, or prostituted to base influences, if the very possibility of such a degradation lay before us, we should sacredly guard ourselves from the remotest danger of such utter prostitution. Only in the healthful, natural use of our powers are we warranted by nature, and only by such use are we benefited and blessed.

4. *In its effect on moral health by weakening self-control.*

It may seem a truism to observe that moral conduct is the result of possessing control over our faculties and passions, yet it is a truism that sadly needs reiterating in these days, when thousands are busily engaged in protracted endeavors to place their faculties under the control of some other power,—when, instead of action being the aim, the mind is systematically reduced to a state of "passive receptivity," and self-control deliberately abnegated. Having no controlling idea within them, no inspiring soul at the helm, many become captivated with the prospect of becoming spiritual watering pots, and distributing to thirsting souls, by a mechanical process, what they instinctively realize they have not the natural means of supplying.

The process of "development" being an unnatural one, and necessarily resulting only in the development of abnormal or morbid faculties, the individual control must be so far weakened. The mind loses its healthful condition of spontaneous activity, and regards every action as the result of "external agencies." It may well be questioned, even whether passivity on our part, and activity on the side of thousands of jacketless men and women "ever with us," could possibly be conducive to morality. Though assuming to be *the* "spiritual philosophy of the nineteenth century," we fail to discover the ghost of evidence that this system possesses even the rudiments of spiritual thought, or influences its followers in their daily conduct to nobler lives.

It is impossible, of course, to lay before the reader any examples to show that this is actually the *result*, yet the fact remains patent to all familiar with the private histories of a large proportion of our constantly-employed *media*, and is still further evidenced in the scandalous stories regarding each other current among *mediums* themselves, and occasionally outcropping in their harangues, as was recently the case, at the "Spiritualists' National Convention," with the physical organism controlled by *Demosthenes*. When a distinguished spiritist lecturer arrives in a town, and after a brilliant lecture on temperance is seen in public resorts, exhibiting himself as a "frightful example" of the need of temperance reform, the excuse of "obsession" is urged to palliate his fault and remove the responsibility. Is a female lecturer left by her husband for lewd and adulterous conduct? "evil spirits" are deemed the cause, and her graceful figure and coquettish ways are as welcome as ever on the rostrum to expound "spiritual truth"! Are families broken up by some ex-reverend whose carnal propensities have overmastered him? we are gravely informed that "certain spirits delight in producing discord"!

Granting that these excuses be correct, it remains a virtual confession that passivity has resulted injuriously to moral health; that moral self-control did not lie within them, and that they were powerless in the hands of unknown agencies, who delight to return and through them gratify their baser passions and propensities, "obsessing" them for their own vile purposes. A spiritist, known in nearly all the Northern States, once remarked to me that he believed he could eat a hearty meal and then be "obsessed" by a "hungry spirit" and eat as much more! The very admission that such a state of things exists, or belief in its *possibility*, is tantamount to confession of the fact alleged.

It has been urged that the result obtained is worth far more than the cost; that we have thereby the fact demonstrated to us that it is possible for those whom we had sadly thought to be dead to return and influence us. Is it not a great, transcendent fact that they live and are still with us? Does not this *knowledge* outweigh all incidental injury to those willing to make "martyrs" of themselves in so holy a cause?

Alas! it is not so apparent. Aside from the grossness of the thought that the attainment of a knowledge of *spiritual* realities *may* be detrimental to moral uprightness in conduct, and is dependent upon physical conditions, we see with sorrow the evidence of complete spiritual paralysis. The soul has become conscious of itself, and sees itself to be a "sublimated" image; it has become an entity, and concerns itself exceedingly as to its ultimate condition. It is no longer a healthful, animating *cause*, but an *effect*. *Spiritual* anatomists dissect it, and give us treatises on *spiritual* physiology. Soul, as an indwelling motive power, unconsciously outworking a purpose in life, by noble and manly endeavor, with firm faith and undoubted reliance in all goodness and nobleness, now lies sick,—has become anxious to know the *why* and *how*. Spiritual digestion has become disordered, and craves for nostrums, and nostrums enough abound! The soul is no longer shrouded in mystery and reverently regarded, but "parceled out into shoplists of what are called 'faculties,' 'motives,' and such like."

We are to have a new religion to meet the soul's dyspeptic cravings; a "religion made easy," with improved mechanism in good working order, whereby we may have "demonstrated to us the existence of other realms wherein we are to reside and progress." Religion, in such sense, becomes but the apotheosis of self! The true, heroic soul will rather answer in the words of one somewhat widely known as a thinker,—

"Let that vain struggle to read the mystery of the Infinite cease to harass us. It is a mystery which, through all ages, we shall only read here a line of, there another line of. Do we not already *know* that the name of the Infinite is GOOD, is GOD? Here on earth we are as soldiers fighting in a foreign land, that understand not the plan of the campaign, and have no need to understand it; seeing well what is at our hand to be done. Let us *do* it like soldiers; with submission, with courage, with a heroic joy. 'Whatsoever thy hand findeth to do, do it with thy might.' Behind us, behind each one of us, lie six thousand years of human effort, human conquest: before us is the boundless time, with its as yet uncreated and unconquered continents and Eldorados, which we, even we, have to conquer, to create; and from the bosom of eternity there shine for us celestial guiding stars.

"'My inheritance how wide and fair!
Time is my fair seed-field, of Time I'm heir.'"

PART II.—THE PHENOMENA.

CHAPTER I.

INTRODUCTORY.

HAVING somewhat critically examined the subject of spiritism as presented in its philosophy, and seen it to be crude and unscientific in its methods, gross and unphilosophical in its teachings, and demoralizing and unnatural in its effects, we might be content to rest. But the mind is not satisfied unless some explanation is presented of the various "manifestations" upon which the philosophy is based. In entering upon this portion of the subject— an examination of the phenomena—we are beset with many difficulties, and frankly confess that, in the present state of psychological science, it does not lie in our power to definitely explain every phenomenon to which spiritists may point; but we may endeavor to point out the false deductions drawn, and show good reason for withholding our belief in the entirely gratuitous assumption that they *must* proceed from disembodied human beings.

Let us carefully investigate the alleged manifestations, and while disclaiming the egotism that would pronounce them well understood, it is still possible to show that, whatever the causes, they can furnish no evidence of the presence of intelligence not in the physical form.

For many years I have carefully investigated the various phenomena presented as "spiritual" in their origin, without prejudice on the one hand, or blind credulity on the other. Soon convinced that the subject was well worth examination, no pains were spared to become acquainted with it in all of its various phases and to endeavor to arrive at just conclusions. In my mind it became established that spirit-communion was a possibility, and that departed friends had the power, under certain conditions, of making their presence known through the physical organism of a living person. While giving assent to this, however, the "communications" were never regarded as reliable: even in the most favorable conditions they seemed to be more or less influenced by the mind of the *medium*. But continued investigation has thoroughly convinced me that my conclusions were premature, and not logical deductions from the phenomena presented. After years of pains-taking and anxious investigation, these former conclusions, drawn from isolated and sporadic "manifestations," were shown to be unwarranted inferences, destitute alike of scientific evidence and philosophical plausibility. To indicate, therefore, the proper manner in which the subject should be studied, and the reasons for denying the inferences based upon the phenomena is the purpose of the remaining pages.

To the spiritist, who already has his complete theory of the universe, and fancies himself in full possession of the key to the mysteries of nature, no appeal is made; it were useless; those already possessing *knowledge* are never students. But the thoughtful, inquiring mind, anxious to know if these marvels do really indicate an extra-material origin, we invite to follow us through the remaining pages, before coming into full possession of the spiritist's "knowledge."

No desire is felt to weaken any one's faith in a future state of being, nor remove anything which may prove a consolation in time of bereavement. The writer has an abiding faith as to the future, a faith that has remained unshaken even under the perusal of countless " communications" purporting to emanate thence, and still cherishes it as one of the soul's most precious possessions. But as men love truth, so do they abhor error, and scout the idea that error ever can be blessed or beneficial to the soul. If error seems for the time to possess consolation, it is because the soul has been content to rest on a lower level ; and the enlargement of its vision, while destroying the supposed consolation, never leaves it destitute. Whatever is truth, is best, no matter whither it may lead us. The soul will instinctively cling to it when once seen, and find consolation and peace only therein.

CHAPTER II.

MENTAL EXALTATION.

The wisest and best of mankind have ever fondly dwelt on the idea that the higher in spirituality we attained, the nearer we were drawn into communion with the spiritual world, and became more receptive to spiritual truths.

"Nearer, my God, to thee,"

and to thy higher realms of thought and existence, nearer to the fount of all truth, and in closer soul-communion with our loved ones gone before, should be the aspiration of every heart and the governing impulse of every mind.

In challenging the "tests of mediumship," the writer would not be understood as denying the existence of a spiritual world, for he is firmly persuaded that his friends who have passed the portals of the tomb have but thrown off the worn-out habiliments of mortality, with its debasing influences, and live on in a wider and higher sphere of action, again to be met when he, as a tardier traveler, shall have groped his way to the journey's end, and the scales of physical existence drop from his sight and permit him to behold what now he cannot dimly conceive. Nay, more : that across the great gulf between this state and that there may have occasionally flashed—to receptive minds *spiritually* attuned—some dim realization of a nobler, holier state of action yet to be attained; that there have been times when children of men have been refreshed with inspiration falling upon their spiritual natures like gentle rain, causing new and loftier thoughts to bud and blossom, so that the fragrance thereof—like musk in the walls of ancient temples—has outlived the ravages of time.

Modern spiritists, however, are not content with this "strait and narrow way" to spirituality, but have improved, as they fondly imagine, upon the original conception; and now they present us with a patent labor-saving apparatus, by which any one may attain to a "knowledge" of spiritual truth by paying from ten cents to ten dollars; the schedule being based not on the net amount of spirituality evolved, but either on the thaumaturgical abilities of the *medium* or the credulity of the "investigator." Not content, moreover, with borrowing a word descriptive of the grandest school of philosophy, ancient or modern, they arrogantly presume to be its special exponents, and, to use the pertinent words of John Weiss, "spell it with a capital S!"

Of all the phases of *mediumship*, the *trance* is the most familiar, in which condition, it is confidently asserted, illiterate men and women, and even children, are capable of lecturing, improvising, singing, dancing, and painting, in a manner far transcending their normal mental powers. Thousands point to these instances of mental exaltation as irrefutable evidences of "spirit-influence," and loudly call upon "mole-eyed science" to explain them or "forever after hold its peace." Similar instances of mental exaltation are familiar to every student in mental philosophy; yet those to whom the human soul is no mystery reiterate this demand. It is undoubtedly proven that these wonderful powers pertain to the mind, and that various causes not due to the ubiquitous "influences" may call them forth; and yet new instances are constantly being paraded in the columns of the spirital press as "demonstrations" of spiritual existence. If we can cite similar phenomena produced by mundane means, then as *direct evidence* of another state of existence this class of phenomena becomes worthless. I therefore proceed to adduce some of the causes known to produce the state of "mental exaltation;" not, however, to claim that all instances may be classified under the heads selected, but to give reason for inferring that still other causes exist, not so well studied and understood.

1. *In mental derangement.*

All competent physicians are familiar with the morbid phenomena of consciousness, and rightly withhold credence in whatever is attested by abnormal or unusual manifestations of it. Hence strong personal consciousness of the reality of any event, under such conditions, carries with it no weight to the intelligent mind. Among the earliest recognized symptoms of organic brain disease, indicating the approach of insanity, softening of the brain, or paralysis, there is often observed a marked exaltation of certain faculties.

Dr. Forbes Winslow, in his work on the "Obscure Diseases of the Brain and Mind," gives some striking illustrations of this fact. He says,—

"Men naturally dull of apprehension, in fact nearly half-witted, exhibit occasionally, both in the early as well as in the advanced stages of insanity, considerable acuteness and capacity."

As examples of this mental acuteness in insanity, we quote from the same work several illustrative cases.

"In the stage of morbid exaltation, the patient frequently exhibits a talent for poetry, mechanics, oratory, and elocution, quite unusual and inconsistent with his education, and opposed to his normal habits of thought. His witty sallies, bursts of fervid and impassioned eloquence, readiness at repartee, power of extemporaneous versification, mechanical skill and ingenuity, amaze those who were acquainted with his ordinary mental capacity and educational attainments. There is an unusual display of vigor of mind, an ability to converse fluently on subjects not previously familiar to his mind, and an aptitude to discuss matters wholly unconnected with his particular situation in life. A quickness of perception, a facility or propriety of utterance quite unusual, becomes in some cases, as the disease progresses, daily more manifest. * * *

"A young gentleman had an attack of insanity caused by rough ill-usage whilst at school. This youth had never exhibited any particular talent for arithmetic or mathematical science; in fact, it was alleged that he was incapable of doing a simple sum in addition or multiplication. After recovering from his maniacal attack, and when able to occupy his mind in reading and conversation, it was discovered that an arithmetical power had been evolved. He was able with wonderful facility to solve several rather complicated problems. This talent continued for several months, but after his complete restoration to health he relapsed into his former natural state of arithmetical dullness, ignorance, and general mental incapacity.

"The wife of a clergyman exhibited, during her paroxysms of maniacal excitement, a wonderful talent for rapid and clever versification. The nurse who was in constant attendance upon the patient was so struck with the phenomenon that she had transcribed, before calling my attention to the fact, a number of verses evidencing poetical powers *of no ordinary* character. The disposition to improvise was manifested mostly at night. After her recovery all capacity for rhyming appeared to subside. I understand that, previously to her illness, she had not exhibited the slightest poetical inclination or ability."

Dr. Benjamin Rush, in his work "On the Diseases of the Mind," writes as follows:

"The records of wit and cunning of madmen are numerous in every country. Talents for eloquence, poetry, music, painting, and uncommon ingenuity in several of the mechanical arts are often evolved in this state of madness. A female patient of mine, who became insane after parturition, in 1807, sang hymns and songs of her own composition, during the latter stage of her illness, with a tone and voice so soft and pleasant that I hung upon it with delight every time I visited her. She had never discovered a talent for poetry or music in any previous part of her life. Two instances of a talent for drawing evolved by madness have occurred within my knowledge; and where is the hospital for mad people in which elegant and complete rigged ships and curious pieces of machinery have not been exhibited by persons who never discovered the least turn for a mechanical art previously to their derangement?"

Pinel, an acknowledged authority on insanity, remarks in this connection that—

"Certain facts appear so extraordinary that they have need of being borne up by the most authentic testimony, in order not to be called into question. I speak of the poetical enthusiasm which is said to have characterized certain paroxysms of mania, even when the verses could nowise be regarded as an act of reminiscence. I have myself heard a maniac declaim, with grace and exquisite discernment, a longer or shorter succession of verses of Virgil or Horace, which had been a long time effaced from his memory. . . . An English author attests that a young girl of a feeble constitution, and subject to nervous affections, had become insane, and during her delirium she expressed herself in very harmonious English verses, though she had before shown no disposition for poetry."

Dr. Abercrombie, in his "Intellectual Powers," mentions the case of a young lady becoming insane, but not violent. "Before her insanity she had been only learning to read, and to form a few letters; but during her insanity she taught herself to write perfectly, though all attempts of others to teach her failed, as she could not attend to any person who tried to do so. She has intervals of reason, which have frequently continued three weeks, sometimes longer. During these she could neither read nor write; but immediately on the return of her insanity she recovers her power of writing, and can read perfectly."

Tasso composed his most eloquent and impassioned verses during paroxysms of insanity. Lucretius wrote his immortal poem when suffering from an attack of mental aberration. Cruden compiled his "Concordance" whilst insane.* Van Swieten relates the case of a young woman displaying the faculty of rhyming, or poetic talent, during her paroxysms of mania, though she had before been occupied with manual labor, and her understanding had never been enriched by culture. Pages might be filled with similar instances, to all but the spiritist susceptible of a psychological solution.

2. *In the use of stimulants.*

Similar effects are sometimes produced by the use of stimulants. In states of depressed energy of the brain, when in a starved and impoverished condition, arising

---

* Winslow: "Obscure Diseases of the Brain and Mind," p. 171. Dendy: "Philosophy of Mystery," pp. 94, 95.

from a deficient supply of blood, the memory becomes impaired, it is well known that vinous stimulants will often act immediately in restoring the memory to its usual activity. Stimulants frequently excite mental faculties, producing that singular phenomenon known as "double consciousness," in which the person apparently leads two lives, forgetting when sober everything transpiring when intoxicated, and *vice versa;* when drunk, with memory only of acts performed or witnessed in former states of intoxication, and when sober with knowledge only of his past sober moments; or, as Mr. Combe has said, a double personality manifests itself in the exhibition of two separate and independent mental capabilities in the same individual; each train of thought and each capability being wholly dissevered from the others, and the two states in which they predominate subject to frequent interchange. An illustration of this curious state of mental action was quoted from Abercrombie in the preceding section.

It has often been asserted that Poe wrote best when under the influence of vinous stimulants. Coleridge's remarkable poetical fragment, " Kubla Khan," was composed while under the influence of opium, and made so deep an impression on his memory that on waking he proceeded to write it down. While engaged in this task he was called away on urgent business requiring his whole attention for a few hours, and on his return found that the remainder of the poem had passed from his memory. " Rousseau's Dream" and Tartini's " Devil's Sonata" owe their birth to brains stimulated by narcotics to flights of fancy and musical expression far surpassing their respective authors' usual powers.

Tartini relates the following anecdote of the origin of his *chef-d'œuvre*, " La Sonata di Diavolo:"

"One night, it was in the year 1713, I dreamed that I had made over my soul to his satanic majesty. Everything was done to my wish: the faithful menial anticipated my fondest wishes. Among other freaks, it came into my head to put the violin in his hands, for I was anxious to see whether he was capable of producing anything worth hearing upon it. Conceive my astonishment at his playing a sonata, with such dexterity and grace as to surpass whatever the imagination can conceive. I was so much delighted, enraptured, and entranced by his performance that I was unable to fetch another breath, and, in this state, I awoke. I jumped up and seized upon my instrument, in the hope of reproducing a portion, at least, of the unearthly harmonics I had heard in my dream, but all in vain; the music which I composed under the inspiration I must admit was the best I have ever written, and of right I have called it the 'Devil's Sonata;' but the falling off between that piece and the sonata which had laid such fast hold of my imagination is so immense, that I would rather have broken my violin into a thousand fragments, and renounced music for good and all, than, had it been possible, have been robbed of the enjoyment which the remembrance afforded me."

Walter Cooper Dendy, in his "Philosophy of Mystery," remarks as follows in this connection:

"The brilliancy of thought may be artificially induced also by various other narcotics, such as the juice of the American manioc, the fumes of tobacco, or the yupa of the Othomacoes on the Orinoco. To this end we learn from a learned lord that even ladies are wont to 'light up their minds with opium, as they do their houses with wax or oil.'

"Indeed, a kind of inspiration seems for a time to follow the use of these narcotics. The Cumæan Sibyl swallowed the juice of the cherry-laurel ere she sat on the divining tripod; and from this may have arisen those superstitious fancies of the ancients regarding the virtues of the laurel, and the influence of other trees, of which I remember an allusion of the excellent author of the 'Sylva:'

"'Here we may not omit what learned men have observed concerning the custom of *prophets* and persons inspired of *old* to *sleep* upon the boughs and branches of *trees*, on *mattresses* and *beds* made of leaves, *ad consulendum*, to ask advice of God. Naturalists tell us that the *Laurus* and *Agnus Castus* were trees which greatly composed the *phrensy*, and did facilitate true *vision*, and that the *first* was specifically efficacious to inspire a *poetical* fury; and *Cardan*, I remember, in his book *de Fato*, insists very much on the dreams of trees for portents and presages, and that the use of some of them do dispose men to visions.'

"During the revery of the opium-eater (not the deep sleep of a full dose, but the first and second stage ere coma be induced), he is indeed a poet, so far as brilliant imagination is concerned."

"Ben Jonson," writes Aubrey, "would many times exceede in drink; Canarie was his beloved liquor; then he would tumble home to bed, and, when he had thoroughly perspired, then to studie."

Dr. Abercrombie states that he attended a gentleman affected with a painful disease, requiring the use of large opiates. On one occasion, the opiates having failed to produce sleep, the gentleman beheld passing before him a number of the celebrities of the day discussing some occurrences of a recent date, and heard their speeches and conversations, some of which were in rhyme, and was able to repeat much of it the next day.

I am acquainted with a lady residing on a farm in Central New York, who, while suffering from a severe attack of the toothache, was induced by her friends to partake generously of alcoholic drinks to "drown the pain;" soon becoming slightly inebriated, she astonished all in the house with her wonderful power of song, singing with a sweetness and pathos truly touching; yet she declared she had never before been able to more than "hum a tune," having had no musical education. This is an instance of spirit-power, direct evidence of the ability of *disembottled* spirits " to manifest in the form."

3. *In slumber.*

We have abundant testimony to the fact of abnormal exaltation of the mental faculties during sleep. Miss Cobbe, in her thoughtful essay on "Unconscious Cerebration," cites several cases of poetical talent being called into existence during slumber. She cites the case of a lady who confessed to have been pondering, on the day before her dream, on the many duties which "bound her to life." This metaphorical allusion became in her sleep a visible allegory. "She dreamed that Life—a strong, calm, cruel woman—was binding her limbs with steel fetters, which she felt as well as saw, and Death, as an angel of mercy, hung hovering in the distance, unable to approach or deliver her. In this most singular dream her feelings found expression in the following touching verses, which she remembered on waking, and which she has permitted me to quote precisely in the fragmentary state in which they remained in her memory:

"'Then I cried, with weary breath,
Oh, be merciful, great Death!
Take me to thy kingdom deep,
Where grief is stilled in sleep,
Where the weary hearts find rest.
* * * * *

" 'Ah, kind Death, it cannot be
That there is no room for me
In all thy chambers vast.
See! strong Life has bound me fast:
Break her chains and set me free.

" 'But cold Death makes no reply—
Will not hear my bitter cry.
Cruel Life still holds me fast,
Yet true Death must come at last,
Conquer Life, and set me free!' "

Miss Cobbe also refers to a lady of her acquaintance who composed a dream-poem which merits attention, as she observes, " seeing that the dreamer in her waking hours is not a poet, and that the poem she dreamed is in French, in which she can speak fluently, but in which she believes herself utterly unable to compose a verse."

Abercrombie ("Intellectual Powers") gives the following interesting instances of mental exaltation in the hours of slumber:

" Dr. Franklin informed Cabanis that the bearings and issues of perplexing political events were frequently unfolded to him in his dreams. A gentleman had been reading an account of the cruelties inflicted by the Turks on the Christians, and in his sleep dreamed that he was a witness of similar scenes, and heard a Turk address the sufferer in some doggerel rhymes, which he was enabled to repeat in the morning.

" A distinguished lawyer of Scotland was occupied in a case which severely taxed his attention and was attended with much difficulty. In his sleep he arose, and, proceeding to his writing-desk, wrote for some time and returned to bed. In the morning he informed his wife he had had a remarkable dream, in which the perplexities of the case had been clearly unraveled, but was unable to recall it. His wife directed him to his desk, where he found a full and luminous opinion on the case, written out in his own hand.

" . . . They [somnambulists] in some cases repeat long pieces of poetry, often more correctly than they can do in their waking state, and not unfrequently things which they could not repeat in their state of health, or of which they were supposed to be entirely ignorant. In other cases, they hold conversations with imaginary beings, or relate circumstances and conversations which occurred at remote periods, and which they were supposed to have forgotten. Some have been known to sing in a style far superior to anything they could do in their waking state, and there are some well-authenticated instances of persons in this condition expressing themselves correctly in languages with which they were imperfectly acquainted."

Sir Isaac Newton solved a subtle mathematical problem whilst sleeping; Condorcet recognized in his dreams the final steps of a difficult calculation, which had baffled his powers during the day; and Cabanis asserts that while engaged on his "Cours d'Etude," Condillac frequently during slumber developed and finished in his dreams a subject which he had broken off before retiring to bed.*

A member of my own family, during the half-unconscious slumber preceding waking, dreamed that she was writing a romance, and each morning she took up the thread of thought where waking from sleep had interrupted it on the previous morning. So interested did she become in the plot and incidents, as they shaped themselves in her mind, without any effort of creative power, that she experienced as much pleasure as if she had been reading some new

---

* Abercrombie : "Intellectual Powers," p. 234.

work of a favorite author. She could retain but a faint recollection of the incidents, and had but a vague impression of the grandeur and sublimity of the style. I recollect a fact in my own experience of somewhat similar nature. I had been deeply interested in researches on the ancient forms of worship, and was very anxious to see a certain work which treated on the religion of the Sabeans, but could not procure it. In my dreams I thought I had obtained the book and eagerly perused its pages. The perusal of the work continued for several nights, and I was much surprised to find how admirably the author handled the subject and how clearly he presented it in all of its aspects. Of course, the eloquent and lucid reasonings of the "learned author" were in perfect harmony with my own conjectures, which, however, had not been arranged into any systematic order, but were existing in my mind in a confused manner.

Dr. Winslow remarks that in this condition "phases of intellectual vigor and states of mental acuteness are developed which were not normal manifestations during waking hours, and did not exist in conditions of healthy thought."

4. *In magnetic somnolency.*

That the "mesmeric" sleep often awakens powers of the mind into action hitherto unknown is now too well established to admit of refutation. The nature of the experiments made upon mesmeric subjects has been such as to absolutely preclude the possibility of longer attempting to account for them on the supposition that the mind of the magnetizer is the sole source of all the intelligence evolved. I admit that in ordinary experiments in "electro-biology" it is undoubtedly true that the mind of the operator determines the action. If he declares the "subject" to be hot or cold, his independent mental action is suspended, and he feels as the mind of the operator wills,—not simply because the operator wills it, but because his own reasoning faculties and will are in abeyance, and he feels that he must be as the other declares. But when the subject enters the deep trance condition, and displays mental powers impossible to account for through control of the imagination, and resulting in actions entirely unsuspected, or giving information unknown to the operator, some other explanation must be resorted to.

In the magnetic state we may observe an exaltation of the mental faculties oftentimes bordering on the incredible. The intellectual faculties seem to be quickened, and questions are frequently discussed which, in waking moments, are far beyond the reach of the normal capability of the mind. Subjects also experience a wonderful development of memory, which, on passing into their normal condition, it is impossible to retain. In addition to the superior coherence of thought sometimes manifested, we discover a power to perceive objects in the deepest darkness, or to hear sounds in distant rooms, sounds which fail to reach the ears of others; and this in cases where the object seen or sound heard is *unknown to the operator or any one present.*

I am aware that those who believe we can receive no impression except by the usual action of the senses will doubt the correctness of these statements; for their theory has no place for such facts as may be brought to substantiate it. That sensation is seated in the senses, rather than in the mind, is an unproven assertion. Thus, the *preparatives* of sensation have been confounded with sensation itself; but, as Sir James Mackintosh has admirably observed, "All the changes in our organs which can be likened to other material phenomena are nothing more than *antecedents and prerequisites of perception*, bearing not the faintest likeness to it: as much outward in relation to the thinking principle as if they occurred in any other part of matter, and of which the entire comprehension, if it were attained, would not bring us a step nearer to the nature of thought."

A few illustrations of the exaltation of faculties in artificial somnambulism, when carefully witnessed and verified by competent persons, are worth more than pages of theorizing or assertions, and will be more welcome to the reader. The Rev. Chauncey Hare Townshend, in his "Facts in Mesmerism," cites many experiments, performed under the most careful scrutiny, evidencing the truth of these statements. From his work the following illustration is quoted:

"Remembering that E. A——, on his father's testimony, had in natural sleep-waking seemed to perceive in total darkness, I was curious to ascertain whether in mesmeric sleep-waking he would manifest a similar phenomenon of sensation. I therefore, having mesmerized him, took him with me into a dark press or closet, of which I employed a friend to hold to the door in such a manner as that no ray of light could penetrate through crevice or keyhole. Then, like the hero of 'The Curse of Kehama,'

'I opened my eyes and I closed them,
And the blackness and the blank were the same.'

"My utmost efforts to see my hand only produced those sparks and flashes which waver before the eye in complete obscurity. Having thus ascertained the perfect darkness of the closet, I drew a card, *at hazard*, from a pack with which I had provided myself, and presented it to the sleep-waker. He said it was so and so. I repeated this to my friend, whom I then told to open the door. The admission of light established the correctness of the sleep-waker; it was the card he had named. The experiments repeated four times gave the same satisfactory result. This peculiar development of vision was, like the other faculties of the sleep-waker, capable of improvement through exercise. At first he seemed unable to read in the dark; then, like a person learning the alphabet, he came to distinguish large single letters which I had printed for him on a card; and at length he could make out whole sentences of even small print. While thus engaged in deciphering letters, or in ascertaining cards, the patient always held one of my hands, and sometimes laid it on my brow, affirming that it increased his *clairvoyance*. He would also beg me to breathe upon the objects which he desired to see. He used to declare that the more complete the darkness was, the better he could exercise his new mode of perception, asserting, that, when in the dark, he did not come to the knowledge of objects in the same manner as when he was in the light. Often when I could not see a ray of light he used to complain that the closet was not dark enough, and in order to thicken the obscurity he would wrap up his head in a dressing-gown which hung in the closet. At other times he would thrust his head into the remotest corner of the press. His perception of color, when exercised in obscurity, sustained but little alteration. He has named correctly the different tints of a set of colored glasses. It was, however, worthy of remark that he was apt to mistake between the harmonic colors, green and red, not only when he was in the dark, but when his eyes were bandaged.

" Many persons can bear testimony to the accuracy of the above experiments; and I refer to the Appendix for proofs that I sought for witnesses and invited scrutiny, feeling that such things as I had to narrate could scarcely be credited on the word of a single person."

In the Appendix we find a number of statements drawn by witnesses to these interesting experiments. M. Van Owenhuysen, of Antwerp, Dr. Foissac, of Paris, Baron de Carlowiz, of Berne, Dr. Wild, of Berne, and others, give interesting descriptions of mesmeric "manifestations" witnessed by them where *clairvoyance* was shown to exist, independently of the minds of those present. Strong testimony would indeed be required to convince us that " E. A——," his best subject, with eyes securely bandaged, could read two hundred pages of print, and even written music; yet it was thoroughly tested. Signor Ranieri, of Naples, and the distinguished Professor Agassiz, relate their experience when under the mesmeric control of Mr. Townshend. Among these letters is one from Dr. Filippi, of Milan, which, being brief, may be quoted in this connection:

" M. Valdrighi, advocate, had his sense of hearing so exquisite and exalted that he could hear words pronounced at the distance of two rooms, the doors of which were shut, although pronounced in a weak and low voice.

"The exaltation of life which is observed in some patients attains such a height, that one of them could see the most delicate and minute objects in the greatest darkness. This is noticed in nervous and very delicate persons."

The case of Miss Brackett, who lived in Providence, R. I., some thirty or forty years since, has been published and commented on by many, though now perhaps forgotten. While totally blind,—the result of an injury,—she manifested *clairvoyant* powers in a high degree. Abundant testimony was collected and published, which now lies before me, showing conclusively that she had the power to correctly *read sealed letters*. The well-known case of Jane Rider, and many others, could also be quoted, if enough had not already been said, as well as instances occurring in the personal knowledge of the writer, where his "subjects" have told him facts which at the time were unknown to him, but subsequently verified. Many cases might be cited of more recent date, but I have preferred to take those where the circumstances were such as to preclude the possibility of deception.

Did space permit, I could cite cases of oratory, philosophical composition, drawing, painting, reading, etc., developed by some of the above causes or others, in each case ability being displayed far transcending the person's natural habits or powers of thought. In natural somnambulism we find the same phenomena; and these two states are too closely related to each other not to be classified under one and the same great law. In the mesmeric "subject" we have an "operator," but in somnambulism the subject and operator are one. A case is narrated in the French Encyclopedia, which occurred under the observation of the Archbishop of Bordeaux. A young minister was a somnambulist, and was observed to rise in the night and "take paper, pen and ink, and proceed to the composition of sermons. Having written a page in a clear, legible hand, he would read it aloud from top to bottom, with a clear voice and proper emphasis. If a passage did not please him, he would erase it, and write the correction, plainly, in its proper place, over the erased line or word. All this was done without any assistance from the eye, which was evidently asleep. A piece of pasteboard interposed between the eye and the paper produced no interruption or inconvenience. When his paper was exchanged for another of the same size, he was not aware of the change; but when a paper of different size was substituted, he at once detected the difference."

Professor Haven relates the following remarkable instances in his Mental Philosophy:

"In a certain school for young ladies—I think in France—prizes had been offered for the best paintings. Among the competitors was a young and timid girl, who was conscious of her inferiority in the art, yet strongly desirous of success. For a time she was quite dissatisfied with the progress of her work; but by-and-by began to notice, as she resumed her pencil in the morning, that something had been added to the work since she last touched it. This was noticed for some time, and quite excited her curiosity. The additions were evidently by a superior hand, far excelling her own in skill and workmanship. Her companions denied, each and severally, all knowledge of the matter. She placed articles of furniture against her door in such a way that any one entering would be sure to awaken her. They were undisturbed; but still the mysterious additions continued to be made. At last her companions concluded to watch without and make sure that no one entered her apartment during the night; but still the work went on. At length it occurred to them to watch her movements; and now the mystery was explained. They saw her, evidently in sound sleep, rise, dress, take her place at the table, and commence her work. It was her own hand that, unconsciously to herself, had executed the work in a style which in her waking moments she could not approach, and which quite surpassed all competition. The picture, notwithstanding her protestations that it was not her painting, took the prize."

Here we have an "accredited manifestation," thoroughly tested by the most approved methods known in "investigating circles," and sufficiently satisfactory to the spiritist to set up a *medium* in business. This case presents as strong " evidence" of a "controlling influence" as most of those recorded in the spiritual journals of our day, and nine out of ten would unhesitatingly accept the work of the somnambule as that of a "spirit-artist." Professor Haven's remarks on this and analogous instances are so pertinent that I shall quote at some length from them:

"How is it, now, that in a state of sleep, with the eye probably fast closed, and the room in darkness, this girl can use the pencil in a manner so superior to anything that she can do in the daytime, with her eyes open and in the full possession and employment of her senses and her will?

" Here are, in fact, several things to be accounted for. How is it that the somnambulist rises and moves about in a state of apparently sound sleep? How is it that she performs actions requiring often a high degree of intelligence, and yet without apparent consciousness? How is it that she moves fearlessly and safely, as is often the case, over places where she could not stand for a moment in her waking state without the greatest danger? How is it that she can see without the eye, and perform actions in utter darkness, requiring the nicest attention and the best vision, and not only do them, but in such a manner as even to surpass what can be done by the same person in any other state under the most favorable circumstances?

* * * * * *

" Another and much more reasonable supposition [than the *automatic* theory] is that the will, which ordinarily in sleep loses control both over the mind and the body, in the state of somnambulism regains, in some way and to some extent, its power over the latter, so that the body rises and moves about in accordance with the thought and feeling that happened at the moment to be *predominant in the mind*. There is no control of the will over those thoughts and suggestions: they are spontaneous, undirected, casual, subject only to the ordinary laws of association; but for the time, whether owing to the greater vividness and force of these suggestions and impressions, or to the disturbed and partially aroused state of the sensorial organism, the will, acting in accordance with these suggestions of the mind, so far regains its power over the bodily organism that locomotion ensues. The dream is then simply acted out. The body rises, the hand resumes the pen, and the appropriate movements and actions corresponding to the conceptions of the mind in its dream are duly performed. . . .

"Whatever theory we adopt, or even if we adopt none, *we must admit*, I think, in view of the facts in the case, that in certain disordered and highly-excited states of the nervous system, as, *e.g.*, when weakened by disease so that ordinary causes affect it more powerfully than usual, it can, and does sometimes, perceive what, under ordinary circumstances, *is not perceptible to the eye or to the ear; nay, even dispenses with the use of eye and ear and the several organs of special sense*. This occurs, as we have seen, in somnambulism, or natural magnetic sleep. We meet with the same thing also in even stranger forms, in the mesmeric state, and in some species of insanity.

"So far as regards the purely mental part of the phenomena, the operations of the mind in somnambulism, there is nothing which is not easily explained. In somnambulism, as indeed in all these states so closely connected,—sleep, dreams, the mesmeric process, and even insanity,—the will loses its controlling power over the train of thought, and, consequently, the thought or feeling that happens to be *dominant* gives rise to, *and entirely shapes*, the actions that may in that state be performed."

In chapter iv. we shall have occasion to investigate the causes of these singular phenomena somewhat more closely: it is enough in this connection to show that such cases do exist. I am well aware that the spiritists will claim that these cases are explicable only on their theory: in fact, the "spirits" inform us, through the *Banner of Light*, that fully one-third of the cases of insanity are really the result of "obsession;" but the intelligent reader would hardly care to read any very lengthy refutation of this antiquated opinion, and I certainly shall not so far trespass on his good nature at present. He would doubt the necessity for controverting a theory which assumes that organic affection of the brain is an essential condition to establish a connection between this world and the next, or that intoxicating drinks render the brain *more passive* and therefore more susceptible to *spiritual* influences. That some can believe that the dreamer is inspired, the opium-eater "obsessed," or that the somnambule's clearness of vision is the result of *spiritual* agents, who return to amaze us by selecting the knave of clubs from a pack of cards, need not surprise us, when we think of the fact that the distinguished French savant M. Paul Broca has collected a library of works published during the present century to sustain the theory that the earth is not spherical, but flat.

In the cases instanced above, the hypothesis of an "influence" operating from the unseen side of life was never once asserted by the persons supposed to be under such control. In most of the instances cited I have chosen those which antedated the advent of our modern polytheism; and as, very singularly, the "unseen influences" forgot to state that they were "spirits," we may reasonably decline to adopt that assumption at this late day.

Thus it appears that "manifestations" as surprising as those witnessed in the "circle" have been recorded as arising from certain states of the nervous system, and, under "right conditions," have occurred without the aid of any mythical "influence" whatever. If affection of the brain can produce them, if stimulants may call them into action, if slumber may arouse faculties of even the existence of which we were unaware, it certainly would be more in accordance with scientific thought to expect that *other causes might* also excite their manifestation. As we shall see hereafter, the powers of the mind are far from being capable of definite limitation, and it were foolhardy to assert that any act of mental exaltation *must* have external spiritual origin.

If a person can play on a musical instrument, or paint, while in a somnambulic or trance state, and—*as we positively know*—possess the power of entering that condition at will without the aid of a "mesmerizer," then as evidence of mediumship for departed spirits it is not only contemptible, but a reflection on the intelligence of those capable of urging it.

CHAPTER III.

"OBSESSION."

1. *Evidence of the senses.*

In the preceding chapter we have seen that the mere fact of an extraordinary exaltation of the mental powers does not in itself furnish us with conclusive evidence that it must necessarily have proceeded from an intelligence distinct from ourselves, and have also seen sufficient reason to refuse the use of the supposition as even a probable cause. In spiritism, however, we find accompanying these states of mental exaltation the claim of distinct personality: the *medium*, in conversation or in writing, while conscious that his acts are not the result of his own normal powers, is also conscious of a claim put forth through him that they are the work of some other intelligent agency. Thus he finds that he not only writes better—though this is not the case universally—than in his normal condition, but that the writing is signed with the name of some deceased person; the power controlling him apparently asserts a distinct individuality.

In considering the claim of "obsession," or the possession of a mortal by a disembodied spirit, we shall find that the evidence is equally weak when submitted to close scrutiny. In examining the arguments adduced in support of this theory, we find the spiritist generally laying great stress on the testimony of his senses. He gravely assures us that he cannot argue the question on the ground of probability, for he has personal knowledge;

he has himself been conscious of being a willing or unwilling instrument in the hands of "spirits;" his eyes have beheld them, his hands grasped them, his ears heard them, or they have controlled him on many occasions, even against his will. Let us examine this evidence of the senses.

In the first place, we have abundant evidence that the senses are not always trustworthy, and may frequently deceive us. Dr. Winslow cites the following passage from a letter addressed to him by a patient: "I am a martyr to a species of persecution from within, which is becoming intolerable. I am urged to say the most shocking things. Blasphemous and obscene words are ever on the tip of my tongue. Hitherto, thank God! I have been able to resist, but I often think I must yield at last; and then I shall be disgraced forever. I solemnly assure you that I hear a voice which seems to be within me, prompting me to utter what I would turn from with disgust if uttered by another. If I were not afraid you would smile, I should say there is no way for accounting for these extraordinary articulate whisperings but by supposing that an evil spirit has obtained possession of me for a time."

The spirital "physician" would at once exclaim that the patient was right so to think; his "Theory of the Universe" readily finds a niche for such facts. But the intelligent physician would regard the matter far differently: to him it would be evidence of disordered mental action, requiring other treatment than a process of "development" and harmonizing circles, if he would not see health entirely destroyed and death rendered inevitable. "These symptoms," remarks Dr. Winslow, "long before they are recognized to be morbid, cause much acute and bitter anguish, concealed suffering, great and unobserved misery in the bosoms of families, often sapping the foundation of domestic happiness. A contest of this nature in an unhealthy but not yet insane mind has continued for a long period unknown, except to the wretched sufferer, before the intellect has succumbed to its baneful and destructive influence."

The spiritist smiles derisively at the charge of disordered mental action, as obviously at fault in many instances, and asserts that his case cannot be so construed, as the different senses *unite* in confirming the distinct individuality of the power claiming to control him. When Copernicus published his theory of the rotundity of the earth, he was met with shouts of derision. "Trust to your senses!" was the response of the deriding populace. When Galileo announced his discovery of Jupiter's satellites, the opponents of "mole-eyed science" again renewed the cry of "Trust to your senses!" This appeal to the senses has been thrown into the faces of all devotees of science in their struggles to reduce discord to order, fancy to reality. And again in our day the same senseless cry is parrot-like repeated, furnishing us, if nothing else, additional evidence of "the power of the mind to resist knowledge." *A dominant idea*, when once in full possession of the mind, may be as productive of delusion as drugs or disease. The studied "development" of abnormal faculties under the impression that the source of the action is due to invisible beings, necessarily shapes the "manifestation," and produces the assertion of distinct individuality on the part of the assumed "influence."

"It is immaterial," says Dr. Draper, in "The Intellectual Development of Europe," "in what manner or by what agency our susceptibility to the impressions of surrounding objects is benumbed whether by drugs, *or sleep*, or disease; as soon as their force is no greater than that of forms already registered in the brain, these last will emerge before us, and dreams *or apparitions* are the result. So liable is the mind to practice deception on itself, that with the utmost difficulty it is aware of the delusion. No man can submit to long-continued and rigorous fasting without becoming the subject of these hallucinations; and the more he enfeebles his organs of sense, the more vivid is the exhibition, the more profound the deception. An ominous sentence may perhaps be incessantly whispered in his ear; to his fixed or fascinated eye some grotesque or abominable object may perpetually present itself. To the hermit in the solitude of his cell there doubtless often did appear, by the uncertain light of his lamp, obscene shadows of diabolical import; doubtless there was many an agony with fiends, many a struggle with monsters, satyrs, and imps, many an earnest, solemn, and manful controversy with Satan himself, who sometimes came as an aged man, sometimes with a countenance of horrible intelligence, and sometimes as a female fearfully beautiful. St. Jerome, who with the utmost difficulty had succeeded in extinguishing all carnal desires, ingenuously confesses how sorely he was tried by this last device of the enemy, how nearly the ancient flames were rekindled. As to the reality of these apparitions, why should a hermit be led to suspect that they arose from the natural working of his own brain? Men never dream that they are dreaming. To him they were terrible realities; to us they should be the proofs of insanity, but not of imposture."

2. *The witchcraft delusion.*

We are not limited, however, to acknowledged cases of disordered mental action for illustrations of the unreliability of the senses when their testimony is claimed as evidence of "spirit-manifestations." Without having recourse to the columns of spirital journals, the pages of history furnish us with numerous instances of supposed "manifestations" by, and intercourse with, invisible beings. Some of these we need to reperuse in order to be better prepared to arrive at a just conclusion.

Let us turn our attention to the records of the sixteenth and seventeenth centuries, when witchcraft was more prevalent in Europe than spiritism has yet become in our land. Witchcraft and spiritism present many points of correspondence. The spiritists themselves generally admit this, and claim that witchcraft was but a form of "spirit-intercourse;" that, finding the effort to open communication between the two worlds only resulting in erroneous views and personal suffering, the sublimated authors of the movement generously consented to forego their endeavors and wait a more favorable opportunity. In that age the supernatural was as readily admitted by the learned as the unlearned; the *existence* of "spirit-intercourse" was undoubted; but our ancestors, with singular obtuseness, could not but regard "obsession" as the work of evil spirits. Readily admitting the spiritual hypothesis, their minds were so clouded with theological dogmas and bigotry as to be unable to imagine that a denizen of the brighter world of spiritual existence *could* desire to return to obsess mortals to dance or leap! Strangely enough, however, we find these bewitched persons claiming in their "obsessed" moments to be influenced by denizens of the pit!

F*

In the early days of the struggle between the Dissenters and the Established Church of England, both parties claimed the power to exorcise spirits who had obtained possession of a mortal *medium*. The memorable case of Richard Dugdale was one of the most remarkable brought forward by the Dissenters. This rustic youth had sold his soul to the devil, in the parlance of the day, in order to become the best dancer in Lancashire. Anxious to relieve him from this demoniacal control, the Dissenters appointed a committee of clergymen, who proposed to exorcise the demon by the usual course of fasting and prayer. They labored for a year, but without accomplishing their purpose. Though unable to exorcise the demon, they grew quite familiar with him, as the following specimen of their railing will exhibit: "What, Satan! is this the dancing that Richard gave himself to thee for? Canst thou dance no better? Ransack the old records of all past time and places in thy memory: canst thou not then find out some better way of trampling? Pump thine invention dry: cannot the universal seed-plot of subtle wiles and stratagems spring up one new method of cutting capers? Is this the top of skill and pride, to shuffle feet and brandish knees thus, and to trip like a doe, and skip like a squirrel? And wherein differ thy leapings from the hoppings of a frog, or the bouncing of a goat, or the friskings of a dog, or gesticulations of a monkey? And cannot palsy shake such a loose leg as that? Dost thou not twirl like a calf that hath the turn, and twitch up thy houghs just like a springhalt tit?"

In how many particulars does this remind me of "circles" in which I have sat with patient waiting for some "test," always promised, yet never realized! Often in the State of Vermont I have heard the shade of Ethan Allen addressed, if not in similar language, yet with equal familiarity; an unusual thump of the table occurring would be greeted with ejaculations of "That's old Ethan!" "How are you, Ethan?" I have sat thus for an hour or more, and at last had my patience rewarded by beholding a member of the company "controlled" to dance for as long a time without apparent exhaustion, and with the others I marveled much, but from a far different reason!

During the year 1871, the *Banner of Light* contained a complimentary notice of the advent of a new *medium*, Mrs. P——, who gave dancing séances "under influence," and was regarded by the faithful as a remarkable *test-medium*. If the assertion of the "influence" through Mrs. P—— is a positive *test*, what shall we call the assertion of his Satanic majesty through Richard Dugdale?

The Established Church also had its cases of Satanic obsessions. The once famous case of the witches of Warbois may furnish us with an instance of the length to which the "evidence of the senses" may go. The witches were a Mother Samuel and her husband, both very old and poor persons, and a daughter, a young woman. The daughter of a Mr. Throgmorton, being taken ill, fancied that Mother Samuel had bewitched her. The other children of the family sympathetically joined in the cry, and "investigation" began. The parents heard the children during their paroxysms carrying on a conversation with some invisible persons, and, when the children recovered, learned from their lips the nature of the remarks made by the "spirits." Sir Walter Scott, in his "Letters on Demonology and Witchcraft," gives us a description of this tragical event, from which the following lively conversation between the "spirit" and one of the girls is taken:

"The names of the spirits were Pluck, Hardname, Catch, Blue, and three Smacks, who were cousins. Joan Throgmorton, the eldest, supposed that one of the Smacks was her lover, did battle for her with the less friendly spirits, and promised to protect her against Mother Samuel herself; and the following curious extract will show on what a footing of familiarity the damsel stood with her spiritual gallant: 'From whence came you, Mr. Smack?' says the afflicted young lady; 'and what news do you bring?' Smack, nothing abashed, informed her he came from fighting with Pluck: the weapons, great cowl-staves,—the scene, a ruinous bakehouse in Dame Samuel's yard. 'And who got the mastery, I pray you?' said the damsel. Smack answered, he had broken Pluck's head. 'I would,' said the damsel, 'he had broken your neck also.' 'Is that the thanks I am to have for my labor?' said the disappointed Smack. 'Look you for thanks at my hand?' said the distressed maiden. 'I would you were all hanged up against each other, with your dame for company, for you are all naught.' On this repulse exit Smack, and enter Pluck, Blue, and Catch, the first with his head broken, the other limping, and the third with his arm in a sling, all trophies of Smack's victory. They disappeared, after having threatened vengeance upon the conquering Smack. . . . Miss Throgmorton and her sisters railed against Dame Samuel; and when Mr. Throgmorton brought her to his house by force, the little fiends longed to draw blood of her, scratch her, and torture her, as the witch-creed of that period recommended; yet the poor woman incurred deeper suspicion when she expressed a wish to leave a house where she was so coarsely treated and lay under such odious suspicion." This unfortunate woman was at length worried into a confession of her guilt, and, with her husband and daughter, was condemned and executed.

In this case the delusion existed in the minds of the persons supposed to be bewitched, and on the testimony of their senses sufficient evidence was obtained to cause the execution of these poor people. Nor need we be surprised at instances of confession on the part of the accused, when we consider the means so often applied for extorting them; but the following case so fully illustrates the folly of relying upon the senses alone in regard to phenomena of this character, that it is commended to the attention of those who delight in collecting "accredited manifestations" to substantiate conjecture.

In the Swedish village of Mohra, about the middle of the seventeenth century, the witchcraft mania had become so general, and involved so many of the inhabitants, that the government sent royal commissioners to investigate the matter and punish the guilty, if such there were. The complaints, attested by persons of all classes, were that certain individuals, instigated by Satan, had bewitched several hundred children, who were daily "obsessed" by demons. In this village alone threescore and ten were seized and imprisoned on this charge, of whom twenty-three confessed to the crime alleged and were executed. In the record of this case we may read, "Fifteen of the children were also led to death. Six-and-thirty of those who were young were forced to run the gauntlet, as it is termed, and were, besides, lashed weekly at the church door for a whole year. Twenty of the youngest were condemned to the same discipline for three days only."

The process adopted by the commissioners was to confront the children with the so-called witches, and listen to the accusations made by the children, who persisted in their tale *notwithstanding* the flogging which awaited them. Three hundred of the children were found who substantially agreed in the following improbable tale: Under instructions from the witches, they were wont to assemble at a cross-way and invoke the presence of the devil, requesting him to convey them to Blockula, a mountain famous for witches' gatherings. The children gave a minute description of his majesty and the methods of transportation provided by him. Here was positive "evidence" equal to that so often related to us in the present time by trance-*mediums*. On the spirital hypothesis, can stronger evidence be conceived than that which convinced these children with the fear of death before their eyes and actually visited upon some of their number? What were learned judges to think, with the spiritual theory firmly established in their minds, when witches and bewitched both united in substantiating the truth of the charges, and gave minute descriptions of the feasts held on the "Devil's Sabbath"? when the children agreed in the statement that they had conversed with the arch-fiend himself, and the witches confessed to having "sons and daughters by the fiends, who were married together, and produced an offspring of toads and serpents"?

If "obsession" was a delusion, then was the method of investigation a false one; if it was real, the public floggings sent the "spirits" off on other business, and benefited society: a conclusion giving rise to another conclusion, as applicable to-day as it was two hundred years since!

Belief in the marvelous and the supernatural was universal, and the reality of these nocturnal gatherings was unquestioned. His infernal highness, we are told, left a very unpleasant odor behind; and we find this fact duly explained in accordance with the spirital science of that time by a Mr. Granville, in terms which, if he were now living, would entitle him to a conspicuous position in the ranks of modern necromancy. "This," he says, "seems to imply the reality of the business, these ascititious particles which he held together in his sensible shape being loosened at his vanishing, and so offending the nostrils by their floating and diffusing themselves in the open air!"

Let us now examine a still different case. The confession of a Scotch witch, Isobel Gowdin, extremely minute in its description of the spirital under-world, is interesting from the fact that it was voluntarily made, and exists judicially authenticated by the signatures of the notary, clergymen, and gentlemen present, was adhered to after frequent examinations, and contains no variation or contradiction in its details. Isobel gave a full and definite account of the pastimes enjoyed by the fiends, their names and personal appearance, the songs sung, the materials of their feasts, and the strange ceremonials of their "Sabbaths." Metamorphoses into the forms of cats, crows, wolves, hares, and other animals, were very common among witches. Isobel relates that having once been sent on an errand by the devil, she assumed the form of a hare, and had the misfortune to meet a pack of hounds. "And I," says Isobel, "ran a very long time, and being hard pressed was forced to take to my own house, the door being open, and there took refuge behind a chest."

After several narrow escapes and new hiding-places, she gained time to say the disenchanting rhyme,—

> "Hare, hare, God send thee care!
> I am in a hare's likeness now;
> But I shall be a woman even now—
> Hare, hare, God send thee care!"

Notwithstanding the severity of the laws, Isobel persisted in these declarations, and even said, "I do not deserve to be seated here at ease and unharmed, but rather to be stretched on an iron rack; nor can my crimes be atoned for were I to be drawn asunder by wild horses."

One more case of a still different nature, and we conclude. On the 8th of November, 1576, Bessie Dunlop was accused of sorcery and witchcraft in Ayrshire, Scotland. She asserted that she obtained all her miraculous knowledge of disease, lost goods, and future events, from the spirit of one Thome Reid, who died at the battle of Pinkie, September 10, 1547, who answered every question which she addressed to him. She described her "spirit" friend as "a respectable, elderly-looking man, gray-bearded, and wearing a gray coat, with Lombard sleeves of the auld fashion. A pair of gray breeches, and white stockings gartered above the knee, a black bonnet on his head, close behind and plain before, with silken laces drawn through the tips thereof, and a white wand in his hand." To render it a complete "test-case," we learn that before his first appearance Bessie had never heard of him, but learned his history from his own lips, and had been sent on errands by him to his son and to others, his relatives, whom he named to her.

One of his old neighbors, to whom Bessie was sent, she was to remind, in proof of the truth of her mission, that he had set out with Reid to go to the battle, which occurred on what was called Black Saturday. She was to recall to his mind that he had desired to pursue a different road, but that Thome Reid had persuaded him to continue the journey, that when they had arrived at the kirk of Dalry, Reid bought a parcel of figs for him and presented them tied up in his handkerchief, and that they parted no more till the fatal field of Pinkie was reached.

Here we certainly find an "accredited manifestation,"

and are moved to listen to the revelations after so convincing a "test." Well might Bessie Dunlop be excused for following the lead of one who had so completely "demonstrated" his existence and continued identity, and incline a willing ear to the tales he told of his "spirit-home." Let us pause to look at that beautiful "land" as it appeared in 1576.

Bessie's ghostly adviser grew so familiar as to invite her to accompany him to the *court of elfland*, where he resided; he promised to take her to the court and introduce her to the queen of the fairies, and on one occasion he took hold of her apron to compel her to go. This generous offer she never accepted, but had frequent opportunities of seeing the fairies when they left their subterranean abode, and on one occasion had the honor of being attended in childbirth by her majesty the fairy queen, who graciously waited upon her in the performance of the duties of a nurse. Notwithstanding her faith in her ghostly protector, his aid proved unavailing to save her from the sad fate of the stake.

Though not herself a visitor to the fairy-land, her countrywoman, Alison Pearson, of Byrehill, in 1588, accepted a similar invitation from a deceased cousin, one William Simpson, and participated in the revelries of that court. Isobel Gowdin, to whose voluntary confession we have referred, in 1662 visited the king and queen of elfland. She gave a very minute description of their majesties and their lilliputian subjects: her knowledge of the habits and customs of that realm was quite extensive, and might furnish some of our seers a new field of investigation.

The accumulated testimony taken at Salem, Mass., is too well known to be dwelt upon in this connection. The evidence which caused a child of five years of age to be indicted in the Commonwealth of Massachusetts, and sufficed to bring a poor *dog* to the scaffold for alleged participation in unholy rites, was every whit as strong and convincing as that of our own day, which seeks to establish the fact of similar phenomena having a like origin, differing, however, from the more ancient epidemic delusion only in attributing the obsessing power to disembodied beings rather than to demons or fairies.

3. *Mental epidemics.*

Dr. Francis Hutchinson said the number of witches and their supposed Satanic intercourse would increase or decrease in proportion to the general belief in the probability or impossibility of such tales. As the spiritist theory prevailed, charges and convictions would be found to augment in a terrific degree ; while under a more doubtful or critical state of the public mind the charges would be disbelieved and dismissed as contemptible ; they would grow less and less frequent, until they ceased altogether to occupy the public mind. So with its modern counterpart, "spirit-obsession;" only in proportion as such tales as grace the columns of the journals of the "spiritual philosophy of the nineteenth century" are believed to be credible, will the testimony increase, and our shelves be in danger of becoming filled with ponderous volumes erroneously called "The History of American Spiritualism."

The sympathy existing between human minds is so great that a delusion, however foolish, can easily find mental soil in which to take root and grow with the rapidity of Jonah's gourd. An illustration of this is found in the old anecdote of a wag stopping in front of an English nobleman's house and intently gazing at one of the bronze lions on the door-step ; his fixed attention soon attracted a crowd of curious idlers. "By heavens! it wags!" he ejaculated, pointing to the lion's tail. Soon the street became impassable, and a large majority of the "investigators" were ready to substantiate the assertion with their solemn oaths. Let us briefly glance over some historic examples of the contagious nature of intense convictions, where they have become epidemic and spread from mind to mind in defiance of common sense and reason.

In the early days of the Christian church, at least as soon as the fourth century, retirement to desert or solitary places became common among Christians. Shut off from all human intercourse, immured in some mountain cave, men sought to win holiness by prayer and penance. This desire to secure salvation through humiliation of the flesh became so general, we are told, that the Christian world was in some danger of becoming depopulated of its believers. At one period the sandy deserts of Egypt alone contained over one hundred thousand religious recluses, one-fourth being females! In every direction throughout the East flocked thousands in mad quest of solitude. In those remote quarters of the earth enthusiasts passed their lives in prayer and demoniacal adventures. Though removed from the carnal cares of the world, they were none the less harassed; for spirits of the damned tormented or tempted them at every opportunity. In vain they redoubled their penances or fasted oftener to conquer these creatures of the imagination: men and women ran naked upon all-fours, associating themselves with the beasts of the field, or, like St. Ammon, rejoiced in being able to assert that they had never seen their bodies uncovered, but the demons haunted them still. Though Didymus never spoke to a human being for ninety years, and Anthony spent a lifetime in extinguishing all lustful desires, the unconquerable spirit-world delighted in presenting before them lascivious forms to still further tempt their constancy. To escape from the embrace of a beautiful spiritual maiden, St. Benedict had to roll himself among thorns. In his presence, it is said, even the bodies of the sinful dead would rise from their graves in the church and depart to bury themselves in unconsecrated ground. Our modern delusion has yet to increase in a wonderful degree, to rival its ancient prototype.

The Crusades furnish us with a striking example of the rapid spread of opinions having no foundation in reason. Under the exhortations of Peter the Hermit and Walter the Penniless, in the eleventh century, thousands of men paved the road through Hungary to the East with a long and ghastly line of whitened bones. Two hundred and seventy-five thousand men, relying upon Divine Providence for material support, and preceded by a goat and a goose, into which the Holy Ghost was asserted to have entered, set out on the mad expedition of capturing Jerusalem from the hands of the infidels. Under the assurance of divine protection, the desire to rescue the tomb of the Saviour became epidemic, and spread to every nook of Christendom. Though the first crusade cost the lives of more than half a million men, a triumph was apparently won in the temporary occupation of the Holy City, where ensued a scene of horror and butchery only possible when men are controlled by delusions of the imagination, and consequently deaf to the voice of reason or the supplications of innocent women and children. A second and third crusade followed before this mania became extinct, showing to what length the mind of man will lead him when " obsessed" by delusion. In those days a ready ear was lent to " accredited manifestations" which abounded on every hand,—"manifestations" of so marvelous a kind (as may be read at length, duly attested, in the lives of the Saints) as to make our itinerant miracle-mongers appear insignificant and puerile.

The witchcraft delusion, as we have seen, furnished "manifestations" attested by all the weight human testimony can give. Though denounced by the Pope as impious, the reality of the phenomena was unquestioned, and consequently the number of cases increased. A bull of Pope Innocent VIII., A.D. 1484, says, "It has come to our ears that numbers of both sexes do not avoid to have intercourse with the infernal fiends, and that by their sorceries they afflict both man and beast. They blight the marriage-bed; destroy the births of women and the increase of cattle; they blast the corn on the ground, the grapes in the vineyard, the fruits of the trees, and the grass and the herbs of the field."

This belief existed even in the most masculine minds. Sturdy Martin Luther was not free from this delusion, and often had long conferences or wearisome wrestlings with the arch-fiend in the solitude of his chamber. So convinced was Luther of the reality of these scenes that we find him confessing to as intimate a knowledge of the inhabitants of the infernal world as Mr. Davis or Judge Edmonds has of the sublimated spherical farmers. "The devil," says Luther, "knows well enough how to construct his arguments, and to urge them with the skill of a master. He delivers himself with a grave and yet with a shrill voice. Nor does he use circumlocution and beat about the bush, but excels in forcible statements and quick rejoinders. I no longer wonder that the persons whom he assails in this way are occasionally found dead in their beds. He is able to compress and throttle, and more than once he has so assaulted me and driven my soul into a corner that I felt as if the next moment it would leave my body. I am of opinion that Gesner and

Œcolampadius came in that manner to their deaths. The devil's manner of opening a debate is pleasant enough, but he soon urges things so peremptorily that the respondent in a short time knows not how to acquit himself."

Though possessing such intimate knowledge of the habits and manners of the denizens of the other world, his resemblance to our modern believers exists in no other particular. Luther was a man of faith; a man who clearly perceived a noble *aim* in life, and steadfastly struggled towards it. Whatever ran contrary to this, whether of this world or of other worlds, was to be manfully met, fought against, subdued. The *aim* was ever kept in view, and when duty called he was always ready to respond: "Were there as many devils in Worms as there are roof-tiles, I would on." With eyes that beheld God's hand in all things, with a soul filled with deep convictions animating his being to manly *doing*, what to him was the tempter's art? No thought of "investigating séances" darkened his mental vision or distracted his fixed gaze from the purpose of life; the warfare of life, to his mind, permitted no dalliance with the embodiment of "undeveloped good," but called for strenuous exertions to guard well his own feet in the road before him, a road rendered luminous by his great and noble soul. A man that could stand in the presence of princes and emperors and proclaim those ever-memorable words,—"It is neither safe nor prudent to do aught against conscience. Here stand I, I cannot otherwise. God help me. Amen!" —is not even to be compared with men of our day who try to subdue the spiritual embodiments of "undeveloped good" with soft words and harmonizing influences. None of those of the harmonizing sort can join in this grand old hymn left us by Luther:

"And were this world all devils o'er,
And watching to devour us,
We lay it not to heart so sore,
Not they can overpower us.
And let the Prince of Ill
Look grim as e'er he will,
He harms us not a whit:
For why? His doom is writ."

Luther, if now living, would find no arch-fiend to battle, and I fear but little controversy would arise with the spirital successors of his majesty, if he waited for one to appear that "excelled in forcible statements and quick rejoinders."

Numerous cases might be referred to in this connection, illustrating the contagious effects of strong convictions when reason is overthrown and delusion sits enthroned in the mind. Every student in history can recall examples, such as the rapid spread of belief in vampirism in Southern Europe during the Middle Ages, the prevalence of flagellation in Italy, and the strange delusion of lycanthropy, or wolf-metamorphosis, in the mountain regions of Austria and Italy. The rise of the sect of Jumpers, in Germany, presents analogous traits to the rise of other sects once flourishing in England and America. Pages might be filled with recitals of deluded enthusiasts participating in the most singular acts, such as running on all-fours, climbing trees, or falling into trances, arising from mental sympathy with those who first exhibited such actions. In another chapter some of these phenomena will be again referred to.

Who now believes that St. Jerome or St. Anthony was visited by lascivious spirital maidens? Who believes that Agnes Sampson, with two hundred other Scotch witches, sailed in sieves from Luth to North Berwick Church to hold a banquet with the devil? Though solemnly asserted in her voluntary confession, yet who lends an ear to the tale told by Isobel Gowdin of visiting the queen of fairy-land in the bowels of the earth, or believes that she was metamorphosed into the form of a hare? Who credits the story that the Hebrew physician of Charles the Bold devoured at one meal, in the presence of the court, a wagon-load of hay, together with its horses and driver? These delusions, though once widespread and fully "accredited," have passed away; yet thousands to-day give full credence to the report of a visit of a learned American judge to a spiritual home, where he socially chatted while the spirital housewife was busily engaged in churning.

Dr. Draper ("Intellectual Development of Europe," p. 412), in commenting upon the witchcraft epidemic, has the following pertinent remarks:

"All the delusions which occupied the minds of our forefathers, and from which not even the powerful and learned were free, have totally passed away. The moonlight has now no fairies; the solitude no genius; the darkness no ghost, no goblin. There is no necromancer who can raise the dead from their graves—no one who has sold his soul to the devil and signed the contract with his blood—no angry apparition to rebuke the crone who has disquieted him. Divination, agromancy, pyromancy, hydromancy, chiromancy, augury, interpreting of dreams, oracles, sorcery, astrology, have all gone. It is three hundred and fifty years since the last sepulchral lamp was found, and that was near Rome. There are no gorgons, hydras, chimæras; no familiars; no incubus or succubus. The housewives of Holland no longer bring forth sooterkins by sitting over lighted chauffers. No longer do captains buy of Lapland witches favorable winds; no longer do our churches resound with prayers against the baleful influences of comets, though there still linger in some of our noble old rituals forms of supplication for dry weather and rain, useless but not unpleasing reminiscences of the past. The apothecary no longer says prayers over the mortar in which he is pounding, to impart a divine afflatus to his drugs. Who is there now that pays fees to a relic or goes to a saint-shrine to be cured? These delusions have vanished with the night to which they appertained, yet they were the delusions of fifteen hundred years. In their support might be produced *a greater mass of human testimony* than probably could be brought to bear on any other matter of belief in the entire history of man; and yet, in the nineteenth century, we have come to the conclusion that the whole, from the beginning to the end, was a deception! Let him, therefore, who is disposed to balance the testimony of past ages against the dictates of his own reason ponder on this strange history; let him who *relies on the authority of human evidence* in the guidance of his opinions now settle with himself what this evidence is worth."

It will not do, however, to congratulate ourselves that all delusions have vanished; for ever and again they reappear in new forms. Though captains do *not* buy favorable winds of Lapland witches, merchants and bankers are found who *do* buy of *mediums* information in regard to speculations in funds! Though the apothecary has ceased praying over his mortar, yet spirital "physicians" advertise powders to which have been "imparted a divine afflatus"! True, no Devils' Sabbath now exists where witches dine with infernal fiends; but "spirit-circles" have taken their place, and *mediums* and spirits eat *apples* in Illinois and *potatoes* in London! The *forms* only have changed; the delusions still linger in the minds of men but happily less dangerous, if not less ridiculous. Our forms of thought have changed, and consequently our mental epidemics are tinged with a different tint. As in these ancient cases, so in the modern, it is equally true, as Professor Haven ("Mental Philosophy," p. 368) has remarked of the operations of mind in somnambulism, that "the thought or feeling that happens to be dominant gives rise to, and entirely shapes, the actions" which constitute their characteristics.

Commerce with *deities* was a common practice in all the ancient polytheistic systems; oracles abounded on every hand, and the communicants purported to be gods. In the Middle Ages *fairies* and *elves* were seen and conversed with, their court visited, and the manners and habits of the citizens carefully noted; an abundant mass of "evidence of the senses" could be adduced to support the belief in the veritable existence of these pigmy people and their controlling influence in human affairs. In the later days of witchcraft delusion the "obsessed" were often quieted by holy water, and frequently on hearing the name of Christ the "influences" rent the air with their shrieks and admitted they were *devils*. In more modern times the same results are seen, but now the devils claim to be departed *fellow-mortals*.

In each case we but see reflected the prevailing superstitious belief of the populace; the mind being "obsessed" with the dominant thought unconsciously shaping the action and determining its characteristics. When deities were thought to be continually around us, the "obsessed" claimed to be controlled by gods; when fairies and elves were believed to abound in every shady forest, these controlling visitants asserted themselves to be such; under a more vivid conception of the literal horrors of hell they were thought to be devils, and such they impiously proclaimed themselves; while in a somewhat more enlightened age, where rationalistic influences have had greater scope, they again reappear under the forms of disembodied mortals, and claim to be Tom, Dick, and Joe. Yet circles have been held and astounding manifestations obtained where all present disbelieved in their spirital origin, and, behold! the "spirits" coincide entirely with the views of those invoking them. Christian spiritalists meet with Christian "spirits" who delight in prayer and biblical exposition and add in no small degree to their convictions; while the less devout find all "spirits" decidedly heterodox in their theology

CHAPTER IV.

UNCONSCIOUS ACTION OF THE BRAIN.

1. *Unconscious cerebration.*

DR. CARPENTER, the distinguished English physiologist, whose labors have accomplished so much towards raising the study of mind from the speculations of metaphysicians to the rank of a new science,—*mental physiology*,—has seriously disturbed the admirers of spiral science by the announcement of his theory of "unconscious cerebration." Common sense Dr. Carpenter defines as *the general resultant of the whole previous action of the mind.* This *resultant*, he holds, is at all times available to the mind, whether we are conscious of the fact or not.

We often receive some important proposition, and decide to wait before forming a definite conclusion on the subject. We consider the subject well, weigh the advantages and disadvantages of the proposed scheme, and still hesitate. If we lay it aside for a few weeks and then reconsider it, we find that in the mean time the mind has referred the matter to our common sense, and gravitates to one side or the other. We then see the whole subject in a clearer light, and more readily arrive at a *sensible* conclusion. This unconscious operation of the brain in balancing for itself all these considerations, in putting all in order, so to speak, towards working out a correct judgment, is what Dr. Carpenter terms "unconscious cerebration."

We see illustrations of this in every day's experience.

The "sober second thought" is the result of such an unconscious operation. In conversation we frequently forget some name or date, and, after vainly endeavoring to recall it, we frequently exclaim, "Well, never mind; I shall think of it presently," and continue the conversation. Often the forgotten word or fact suddenly presents itself to our consciousness without previous warning, and we avail ourselves of it without pausing to thank the silent messenger that had hunted it up from the storehouse of memory at our bidding. In cases of what are familiarly termed "absence of mind" we may see illustrations of the same fact. In walking, a man may become absorbed in deep thought, and take no note of his whereabouts; but the mind is not "absent" in the sense the term implies, for it guides him with accuracy through the jostling crowd of which his conscious self has taken no notice. He has turned the usual corners, avoided the carriages in crossing the crowded thoroughfares, and arrives with safety at the end of his journey. Dr. Carpenter has given numerous illustrations of unconscious cerebration, two of which are worthy of quotation, as they place the subject in so clear a light:

"The manager of a bank in a certain large town in Yorkshire could not find a key which gave access to all the safes and desks in the bank. This key was a duplicate key, and ought to have been found in a place accessible only to himself and to the assistant manager. The assistant manager was absent on a holiday in Wales, and the manager's first impression was that the key had probably been taken away by the assistant in mistake. He wrote to him, and learned to his own great surprise and distress that he had not got the key, and knew nothing of it. Of course, the idea that the key which gave access to every valuable in the bank was in the hands of any wrong person was distressing. He made search everywhere, thought of every place in which the key might possibly be, and could not find it. The assistant manager was recalled, both he and every person in the bank was questioned, but no one could give any idea of where the key could be. Of course, though no robbery had taken place up to this point, there was the apprehension that a robbery might be committed after the storm, so to speak, had blown over, when a better opportunity would be afforded by the absence of the same degree of watchfulness. A first-class detective was then brought down from London, and this man had every opportunity given him of making inquiries. Every person in the bank was brought up before him; he applied all those means of investigation which a very able man of this class knows how to employ, and at last he came to the manager and said, 'I am perfectly satisfied that no one in this bank knows anything about this lost key. You may rest assured that you have put it somewhere yourself, and you have been worrying yourself so much about it that you have forgotten where you put it away. As long as you worry yourself in this manner you will not remember it; but go to bed to-night with the assurance that it will be all right, get a good night's sleep, and in the morning I think it is very likely you will remember where you have put the key.' This turned out exactly as it was predicted. The key was found the next morning in some extraordinarily secure place, which the manager had not previously thought of, but in which he then felt sure he must have put it himself."

In this case even the most persistent believer in the marvelous would hardly have the impertinence to suggest a super-mundane cause to account for the finding of the key. Following the advice of the detective, the banker dismissed all anxiety from his mind, and became, in our modern jargon, in a "state of passive receptivity." In this condition his own mental faculties sufficed to restore the forgotten fact to his consciousness. If in his slumber that night some "guardian spirit," or the form of some deceased friend, had appeared before him in his dreams and told him where the key had been secreted, ignorance of the laws of mental physiology might have claimed the *vision* as an "accredited manifestation." But the same explanation would have sufficed even in that case. In dreams we have illustrations of unconscious brain-work; flights of fancy, or the weaving of events into some marvelous story, go on during sleep in the brain of even the dullest mortal, who is never conscious of fancy or imaginative powers in his waking moments. Addison says, in his *Spectator*, "There is not a more painful act of the mind than that of invention. Yet in dreams it works with that care and activity that we are not sensible when the faculty is employed."

Many dreams are related by the superstitious, wherein missing wills or deeds have been found through the interposition of some friendly apparition which thus appeared in the hours of sleep and "impressed" the required fact on the mind. In such cases we may safely assume that "unconscious cerebration" is the friendly sprite that ransacks the galleries of memory and sets before us the forgotten fact in some fanciful frame of its own manufacture.

These remarks will aid us in better understanding the other illustration yet to be cited from Dr. Carpenter, who gives as his authority a well-known clergyman, the Rev. John De Liefde. A student had been attending a class in mathematics, and the professor had said to his class, "'A question of great difficulty has been referred to me by a banker,—a very complicated question of accounts, which they themselves have not been able to bring to a satisfactory issue, and they have asked my assistance. I have been trying, and I cannot resolve it. I have covered whole sheets of paper with calculations, and have not been able to make it out. Will you try?' He gave it as a sort of problem to his class, and said he would be extremely obliged to any who would bring him the solution by a certain day. This gentleman tried it over and over again. He covered many slates with figures, but could not succeed in resolving it. He was a little put on his mettle, and very much desired to attain the solution; but he went to bed, on the night before the solution, if attained, was to be given in, without having succeeded. In the morning, when he went to his desk, he found the whole problem worked out in his own hand. He was perfectly satisfied that it was his own hand; and this was a very curious part of it,—that the result was obtained by a process very much shorter than any he had tried. He had covered three or four sheets of paper in his attempts, and this was all worked out on one page, and correctly worked, as the result proved. He inquired of the woman who attended to his rooms, and she said she was certain no one had entered his room during the night. It was perfectly clear that this had been worked out by himself."

During the day his anxiety to accomplish the result prevented the unconscious action of the brain, which accomplished the task so readily after he had desisted; and, while his mind is supposed to be *dormant*, the difficult task is correctly accomplished. In many of the instances cited in the last two chapters we find this view alone to be the key which can open the door and shed light on their seeming mysteries. The case alluded to in a previous chapter, of a girl rising in the night and passing hours at her easel, engaged in painting, and with such superior skill, is a striking illustration of unconscious brain-action. Nearly every reader can recall some instances where persons have shown the power of waking at any given hour in the night, while others are able at any moment, waking from a sound sleep, to tell the hour with almost unfailing accuracy.

The following incident, known to the writer, will also furnish us with another illustration of this curious power. Mrs. D——, a lady residing in an Eastern city, was one evening sitting quietly in her chamber, reading. Her husband was absent, and she was alone in the house, but had no thought of fear. Suddenly, springing from her chair, and dropping her book, she ran to the door and hastily turned the key in the lock, though why she did so she was unable to say. Almost immediately she saw the knob noiselessly turn and the door tried; and to her inquiry, "Who's there?" a strange voice replied with some inquiries. She resolutely refused all appeals to open the door, and the man was forced to retire. Looking from her window, she saw three men, all strangers, leave the house. There was a considerable sum of money in the room, and she has no doubt their intention was robbery. In this case "unconscious cerebration" at once gives us the clue to the solution of the enigma. Sitting quietly, with her attention absorbed in her book, the stealthy steps of the intruders were heard, and yet not sufficiently to impress her conscious self with the fact,—as we often hear the clock strike, though the mind is too absorbed to permit of the impression being transmitted to our conscious thoughts. The impression transmitted to her brain gave rise to the unconscious start and locking of the door, to guard against some unrealized yet impending danger, in precisely the same manner as the student was moved to rise in his sleep and work out the problem.

I use the term *unconscious* in its popular sense, as absent from our present state of consciousness. Strictly speaking, it may well be questioned whether the mind is ever unconscious; but a treatise on mental philosophy is not the task I have here assigned to myself, and the use of terms in the above sense is sufficiently explicit for the purpose in view. During abstraction or slumber, the senses being *closed* to the objective world, no sensations are received and transmitted to the cerebrum, and its activity at these times must be carried on independently of the sensorium. In dreams, and in partial intoxication from spirits or narcotics, the cerebrum unconsciously works from the stock stored up by memory within its own domain. Dr. Carpenter having first introduced the term "unconscious cerebration" to elucidate these unnoticed workings of the mind, and more prominently than others having associated his name with this theory, I shall again quote from him, that his views may be clearly stated.

In his lecture before the Royal Institution, March 1, 1868, he defines the relations between the cerebrum and the sensorium as made known by scientific research. The cerebrum, according to him, is "a superadded organ, the development of which seems to bear a pretty constant relation to the degree in which intelligence supersedes instinct as a spring of action. The ganglionic matter which is spread out upon the surface of the hemispheres, and in which their potentiality resides, is connected with the sensory tract at their base (which is the real centre of conveyance for the sensory nerves of the whole body) by commissural fibres, long since termed by

Reid, with sagacious foresight, 'nerves of the internal senses,' and its anatomical relation to the sensorium is thus precisely the same as that of the retina, which is a ganglionic expansion connected with the sensorium by the optic nerve. Hence it may be fairly surmised,— 1. That as we only become conscious of visual impressions on the retina when their influence has been transmitted to the central sensorium, so we only become conscious of ideational changes in the cerebral hemispheres when their influence has been transmitted to the same centre. 2. That as visual changes may take place in the retina of which we are unconscious, either through temporary inactivity of the sensorium (as in sleep), or through the entire occupation of the attention in some other direction, so may ideational changes take place in the cerebrum, of which we may be unconscious for want of receptivity on the part of the sensorium, but of which the results may present themselves to the consciousness as ideas elaborated by an automatic process of which we have no cognizance."

In his "Human Physiology" (p. 588) he dwells at some length on this subject: "Most persons who attend to their own mental operations are aware that when they have been occupied for some time about a particular subject, and have then transferred their attention to some other, the first, when they return to the consideration of it, may be found to present an aspect very different from that which it possessed before it was put aside; notwithstanding that the mind has since been so completely engrossed with the second subject as not to have been consciously directed towards the first in the interval. Now, a part of this change may depend upon the altered condition of the mind itself, such as we experience when we take up a subject in the morning with all the vigor which we derive from the refreshment of sleep, and find no difficulty in overcoming difficulties and in disentangling perplexities which checked our further progress the night before, when we were too weary to give more than a languid attention to the points to be made out, and could use no exertion in the search for their solutions. But this by no means accounts for the *entirely new development* which the subject is frequently found to have undergone when we return to it after a considerable interval; a development which cannot be reasonably explained in any other mode than by attributing it to the intermediate activity of the cerebrum, which has in this instance automatically evolved the result without any consciousness. Strange as this phenomenon may at first sight appear, it is found, when carefully considered, to be in complete harmony with all that has been already affirmed respecting the relation of the cerebrum to the sensorium, and the independent action of the former; and, looking at all these automatic operations by which results are evolved without any intentional direction of the mind to them, in the light of reflex actions of the cerebrum, there is no more difficulty in comprehending that such reflex actions may proceed without our knowledge, so as to evolve *intellectual* products when their results are transmitted to the sensorium and are thus impressed on our consciousness, than there is in understanding that impressions may excite muscular movements through the 'reflex' power of the spinal cord, without the necessary intervention of sensation. In both cases, the condition of this mode of independent operation is that the *receptivity* of the sensorium shall be suspended *quoad* the changes in question, either by its own functional inactivity, or through its temporary engrossment by other processes."

For the facts and reasons set forth above, we are justified in ascribing to the unconscious brain the following powers:

I. It can control the various organs of the body, enabling us to read, write, draw, play on instruments, or discourse, frequently in a manner not justified by our normal acquirements;

II. It can ransack the storehouse of memory and bring to our conscious self words or facts sought for in vain in our conscious moments;

III. It can weave common impressions into terrible romances or beautiful pictures, and can perform the exceedingly difficult task of mental arrangement and logical division of subjects;

IV. It can tell the hour in the night without a timepiece.

2. *All impressions permanent.*

Before we apply these mental powers to the phenomena presented by trance *test-mediums*, it will be necessary for us first to examine another point in mental physiology, in order that our means may be more ample in attempting to resolve so difficult a problem. A few words must be said on the subject of memory and its retentive hold of *every* impression transmitted over the nerves of sensation. Retentiveness is not a *quality* of memory, thereby implying its existence in a greater or less degree, but retentiveness *is itself* memory. The power to recall a past impression to consciousness may be wanting, but it by no means follows that the desired fact is lost to memory. Our control over past impressions is not a direct one: if we desire to recall a certain date, for instance, it is because it is not present in consciousness; if it were, there would be nothing to recall. Finding ourselves unable to recall the desired impression, we resort to comparisons, or associations, or some other suggestive process by which the desired fact may be brought into consciousness. Our inability by no means proves that the impression is *lost* beyond recovery, or obliterated, but that our control over it is lost. The impression remains, and at some future time may present itself to consciousness either with or without a mental effort on our part.

Many cases are on record showing the power of the mind, in many cases, of recalling impressions at will. "Cyrus, it is said, knew the name of every officer—Pliny has it, of every soldier—that served under him. Themistocles could call by name each one of the twenty thousand citizens of Athens. Hortensius could sit all day at an auction, and at evening give an account from memory of everything sold, the purchaser and the price. Muretus saw at Padua a young Corsican, says Mr. Stewart, who could repeat thirty-six thousand names in the order in which he heard them, and then reverse the order and proceed backward to the first. Dr. Wallis, of Oxford, on one occasion, at night, in bed, proposed to himself a number of fifty-three places, and found its square root to twenty-seven places, and, without writing down numbers at all, dictated the result from memory twenty days afterwards. It was not unusual with him to perform arithmetical operations in the dark, as the extraction of roots, *e.g.*, to forty decimal places. The distinguished Euler, blind from early life, had always in his memory a table of the first six powers of all numbers from one to one hundred. On one occasion two of his pupils, calculating a converging series, on reaching the seventeenth term, found their results differing by one unit at the fiftieth figure, and, in order to decide which was correct, Euler went over the whole in his head, and his decision was found afterwards to be correct. Pascal *forgot nothing* of what he had read, or heard, or seen. Menage, at seventy-seven, commemorates, in Latin verses, the favor of the gods in restoring to him, after partial eclipse, the full powers of memory which had adorned his earlier life."*

Dr. Kitto says, "I retain a clear impression or image of everything at which I ever looked, although the coloring of that impression is necessarily vivid in proportion to the degree of interest with which the object was regarded. I find this faculty of much use and solace to me. By its aid I can live again at will in the midst of any *scene or circumstance* by which I have been once surrounded. By a voluntary act of mind I can in a moment conjure up the whole of any one out of the innumerable scenes in which the slightest interest has at any time been felt by me."†

These are instances of extraordinary memory; yet the marvel exists only in the power to recall so easily what the mind has once entertained. The same great library exists in each one of us, but we are not all privileged to command its contents at will. But will is not the only cause which brings up before us the events of which we have been once cognizant. Impressions made on the mind in childhood, and, as we say, forgotten in afterlife,—impressions of which we remain ignorant even when we are told of the circumstances by others,—may be brought on the ever-shifting stage of consciousness by some event where the will is not employed. All know that persons resuscitated from drowning sometimes assert that in the short space of time in which they are in the water, every act of their lives seems to be simultaneously restored to consciousness. Miss Cobbe gives the fol-

---

* Haven : "Mental Philosophy," p. 127.
† Moore: " Body and Mind," p. 206.

lowing instance of unconscious memory in one of her thoughtful essays: "Under some special excitement, and perhaps inexplicably remote association of ideas, some words which once made a violent impression on us are remembered from the inner depths. Chance may make these either awfully solemn, or as ludicrous as that of a gentleman shipwrecked off South America, who, as he was sinking and almost drowning, distinctly heard his mother's voice say, 'Tom! did you take Jane's cake?' The portentous inquiry had been addressed to him forty years previously, and (as might have been expected) had been wholly forgotten."

Disease often brings trooping before the consciousness long-forgotten events: sometimes we repeat in fever long trains of phrases which we have once heard, and which may *not* have made a *vivid impression* at the moment. Instances are on record where persons have repeated either living or dead languages which they had once heard, but of the meaning of which they were entirely ignorant. The case of a German servant-girl, cited by Coleridge, is frequently narrated. This girl, while at her work in a room adjoining her master's study, had heard him reading aloud from the Hebrew Bible, and in the delirium of fever in after-years, in other surroundings, she astonished those around her by repeating these Hebrew sentences that had once been uttered in her hearing. The expression "going in one ear and out the other" is true only of our present state of consciousness: the mind itself is more than any state of consciousness, it embraces them all.

Dr. Abercrombie relates the following instances: "A lady, in the last stage of a chronic disease, was carried from London to a house in the country; there her *infant* daughter was taken to visit her, and, after a short interview, was carried back to town. The lady died a few days after, and the daughter grew up without any recollection of her mother, till she was of mature age. At this time she happened to be taken into the room in which her mother died, without knowing it to have been so; she started on entering it, and, when a friend who was along with her asked the cause of her agitation, replied, 'I have a distinct impression of having been in this room before, and that a lady, who lay in that corner and seemed very ill, leaned over me and wept.'

"A boy, at *the age of four*, received a fracture of the skull, for which he underwent the operation of trepan. He was at the time in a state of *perfect stupor*, and, after his recovery, retained no recollection of the operation. At the age of fifteen, during the delirium of a fever, he gave his mother a correct description of the operation and the persons who were present at it, with their dress and other minute particulars. He had never been observed to allude to it before, and no means were known by which he could have acquired the circumstances which he mentioned."

Similar instances could be quoted, but I restrict myself to one or two more illustrating the same fact under other circumstances. Miss Martineau gives an instance of a congenital idiot who had lost his mother before he had reached *two years of age*, and of course before he was able to retain any consciousness of her person. Yet at the age of thirty, when dying, he "suddenly turned his head, looked bright and sensible, and exclaimed, in a tone never heard from him before, 'Oh, my mother! how beautiful!' and sunk round again—dead."

Dendy, in his "Philosophy of Mystery," gives a curious instance of memory occurring in the state of somnambulism. "We have heard of one more interesting case, in which the somnambule, remembering that he had made errors in his writing, traced, on a blank paper substituted for that written on, the corrections *in the very places corresponding to the erroneous writing.* And that here was memory was proven in this, that during the time his eyes were shut, the pen was dropped on the very spot where the inkstand stood; but, this being removed, no ink was obtained, and the writing was blank."

A number of anecdotes might be quoted of persons in abnormal sleep repeating violin-, guitar-, or piano-playing which they had heard in former years. This is still more wonderful; for not only are the sounds remembered, but the capacity to reproduce them on the instrument is also developed. A case of this nature a few years since went the rounds of the press as a marvelous phenomenon. It was stated that a child from the mission-school in New York had been adopted by a gentleman and his wife in the West. The child was a delicate girl, and they soon grew very much attached to her. One night, after having retired, they were very much surprised to hear on the piano in their parlor one of the most difficult pieces of a distinguished German composer. Their first impression was that visitors had called, intending a "surprise;" but on dressing and descending to the parlor, their astonishment was augmented at seeing this little girl seated at the piano. After playing a few choice selections, she arose, gracefully bowed, and withdrew. Nearly every night this scene was repeated, and soon grew into an expected occurrence. The girl was entirely ignorant of her part in the transaction, and was not aware that she had left her bed. After a few nights' silence, she turned to her admiring auditors when she had finished, and, gravely speaking, asserted that she was the mother of the child whose form she was using, and took that method of developing her daughter into a musician. The poor child grew more and more delicate, and soon died.

On the spirital hypothesis we must admit that her declining health made her susceptible to her mother's influence; but this would be admitting *disease* as a condition or aid to mediumship. Again we fail to see how a process which was plainly destroying the health of the child could be instrumental in developing her into a musician, she in the mean while remaining in entire ignorance of the existence of such a process. Inquiries were made after her death, and it was ascertained that she was the daughter of a widow, a very accomplished music-teacher, who had died in great privation and left the daughter at the age of five years to the charity of strangers.

Mental pathology alone furnishes us with the clue to this enigma. We may be warranted in asserting that every piece played by the child had been played in her hearing by her mother in her childhood, and probably listened to by her with wonder and delight. In her diseased condition we find but another instance of unconscious memory, so often reappearing as we draw near to the portals of death. In her orphaned condition and delicate health, what more natural than that the comforts of a home should lead her thoughts to dwell on her mother, and fondly try to recall some faint recollection of her form and features, leading her perhaps to believe that her mother was watching over and guiding her steps? This morbid thought, perhaps assisted by some association of ideas connecting her mother with the playing, became *dominant* in her abnormal state at the piano; and on the ejaculations of a dreaming child in a walking sleep, we are called upon to accept as "positive evidence" the fact of her mother's presence *in propria persona*.

Not to multiply illustrations of similar cases, we may now augment our conclusions in regard to the unconscious brain with these additional powers:

V. It can remember impressions made upon the senses at almost any period of life in our conscious moments;

VI. It can, under certain conditions, reproduce impressions made on the senses during infancy, or while in an unconscious state;

VII. It can manifest *all* the powers of the conscious brain, as in the state of double consciousness, leaving us in doubt as to which is the conscious and which the unconscious condition;

VIII. It can "manifest" mental powers far superior to those of its normal condition, and claim a distinct individuality for itself.

3. *Mental telegraphing and prevision.*

We are told, however, that *mediums* give us "tests of spirit-presence" inexplicable upon any theory of unconscious cerebration. A stranger visiting the city is often urged to call upon a *medium*, and, doing so, is surprised to hear of events known only to himself, the names of friends no longer living, with their age and the date of their demise. Struck with astonishment by these marvelous facts, he eagerly listens to the dull commonplaces purporting to be communications from the denizens of the heavenly world. Assured, as we have been by our philosophers, that all our fundamental ideas are derived from impressions transmitted by the senses alone, he may well be startled on hearing such revelations from the lips of an entire stranger, and the general result of such previous teaching is that thousands are led to believe that invisible beings must be assumed to account for these phenomena, and then collect records of the phenomena to use as *evidence* of the truth of the assumption. Once firmly convinced, they are prepared to join the spirital ranks, and, "arguing in a circle," smile derisively at "mole-eyed science." There *must* be a "spirit-world," or these singular phenomena would be left in the awkward predicament of not being understood; it is the only hypothesis which accounts for the facts. Then, in the next breath, they *know* there is a "spirit-world," because they have communicated with persons now dwelling there.

The question forced upon us is, How can the *medium* obtain this accurate knowledge without the aid of invisible "intelligences"? In accordance with the plan pursued heretofore in these pages, permit me to cite a few "marvelous facts," "accredited manifestations" in mental philosophy, to serve as a groundwork upon which any explanation whatever must be based. It is not necessary that we should be able to "explain" all the marvelous phenomena of mind; it will suffice to show that mental philosophy presents as "marvelous phenomena" as the circle-room of any *medium*; and if these cannot be "explained" by the spirital theory of invisible agencies, but pertain to the mind itself, their consideration is essential before asserting that "spirit-presence" is a *necessary* assumption.

In the first place, I desire to give instances illustrative of the *fact* that ideas are communicated from mind to mind without the conscious use of the physical organs of sight, hearing, or speech. This communication of thought may take place by direct effort of the will, or it may be by unconscious action. The phenomena of mesmerism, of which some illustrations have been given, furnish us with many instances of the transmission of thought produced by the will of the operator. Prof. W. D. Gunning, in his admirable essay, "Is it the Despair of Science?" relates a case which substantiates this position. He says an eminent physician of Philadelphia went one day to hear an "inspirational" *trance-medium,* and told him the following facts. "The medium was a frail, sensitive woman, and one of the most successful speakers of her class. The doctor went to try an experiment. He wrote out a very short lecture, memorized it, and tore up the manuscript. When he entered the hall, the audience had assembled, and the medium sat on the platform. He fixed his eye on her, and, by a strong effort of will, caused her to rise and walk forward to the desk. Then he thought over his lecture, keeping his will on her, and *she delivered it, word for word,* as the words rose up in his mind. The woman intended no deception. She knew that she was not speaking her own thoughts, and, very naturally, she referred the control to a spirit."

Dr. Brittan, an able and eloquent exponent of the "spiritual philosophy of the nineteenth century," in his work on "Man and his Relations," devotes an entire chapter to "Mental Telegraphing," and relates many instances, coming under his own immediate observation, where persons once having been under magnetic control were subsequently influenced by him at a distance of miles. All familiar with what is called magnetic influence must have observed similar instances not unfrequently. Probably no "science" has been based so much on delusion as the so-called "science of mesmerism;" yet, notwithstanding the absurdity of its claims, its phenomena have shown that thought *may* be transmitted without the use of the usual modes afforded by the senses.

Again, thought may be communicated from mind to mind without any conscious effort on the part of either person. I am acquainted with a lady who for a long time was frequently "impressed" with the thoughts of others before they were spoken, frequently answering persons before the question had been orally expressed, though the question related to matters which rendered any guess-work or "association of ideas" utterly impossible. On one occasion a young lady entered the room where she was sitting, about ten o'clock in the evening, and, before the former had closed the door, she was greatly surprised to hear her exclaim, in a jocular manner, "You cannot have any of my quince-sauce!" The young lady admitted that this was what she had come for. On no previous occasion had she expressed any desire for the article in question, which had been prepared a number of months before, and she came at that time, as she expressed it, from "a sudden whim." Scores of similar instances which have occurred in my presence might be given. The well-known spiritist, "Rev." Chauncey Barnes, whose zeal has never outstripped his credulity, regards himself as "highly mediumistic," *because* he can inform you what article of furniture, book, or other object you have touched, or mentally selected, while he was out of the room. These "tests" are gravely paraded in the various towns and cities of the Union—for *where* has he not been?—before awe-struck investigators as wonderful evidences of *mediumistic* powers! I knew a worthy gentleman, now deceased, who was peculiarly susceptible to mental impressions, frequently foretelling the arrival of guests, however unexpected their coming had been; and on more than one occasion he was conveniently absent when a "dun" was meditating a descent on the house.

Presentiments furnish us with other illustrations of this singular faculty of the mind. A case frequently cited is that of Governor Marcy's daughter, who had a fearful presentiment on the morning of her father's death, and felt confident that some terrible calamity brooded over her. A telegram soon confirmed her foreboding. Another instance, to be found in several textbooks on mental philosophy, is that of the sister of Major André, who, it is said, dreamed of her absent brother, one night, as arrested and on trial before a court-martial. "The appearance of the officers, their dress, etc., was distinctly impressed on her mind; the room, the relative position of the prisoner and his judges, were noticed; the general nature of the trial, and its result, the condemnation of her brother. She woke deeply impressed. Her fears were shortly afterwards confirmed by the sad intelligence of her brother's arrest, trial, and execution, and, what is remarkable, the facts corresponded to her dream, both as respects the time of occurrence, the place, the appearance of the room, position and dress of the judges, etc. Washington and Knox were particularly designated, though she had never seen them."

However it may be with the above dream, there are others quite as remarkable which are fully "attested." Dr. Moore, in his work on "Body and Mind," narrates the following as having occurred under his own observation. A friend of his dreamed that he was amusing himself, as he was in the habit of doing, by reading the inscriptions on the grave-stones in a country churchyard. While thus engaged, he saw with great surprise the name, and date of death, of an intimate friend with whom he had that very evening been engaged in conversation. Nothing more was thought of the dream till some months afterwards he received intelligence of his friend's death, which, singularly enough, corresponded in date with that dreamed of as being inscribed on the tombstone.

An instance occurred in my presence some years since which may be put on record as an "accredited manifestation," as the persons concerned are still living and distinctly remember the circumstance. In the month of November, 1859, I was escorting a lady home from an evening entertainment, and in passing the windows of her house, before reaching the door, she declared she saw a body laid out on the sofa, covered with a sheet. On entering the house, we learned that a gentleman temporarily stopping there had that evening received a telegram informing him of the death of his only son, who had left the city a week previous in good health. No person was in the room except the lady's mother, and the death was entirely unexpected, as no intelligence of his sickness had been received.

The father of the Rev. C. W. Cushing, formerly president of a collegiate institute in Vermont, was for many years a sexton, and not unfrequently told his family he should not go to his usual labor, for he would be called upon to prepare a grave: this would prove true, though he had no information of the sickness of the person deceased. Another gentleman living in Vermont assures me that upon entering a room where persons are engaged in conversation, he frequently "gets the thread of their remarks" though not a word has reached his ear.

Can we suppose that a "spirit" whispered to my lady friend that her visitor wished quince-sauce? that the "Rev." Chauncey Barnes is attended by a "spirit-band" to astonish rustics? that "invisibles" tell us of the approach of duns, or that a grave must be dug? that they hover around us in dreams to foretell future events or far-distant occurrences? that they delight in "impressing" our minds with the misfortunes of acquaintances or the conversation of gossips? How did Andrew Jackson

Davis obtain the thoughts expressed in "Nature's Divine Revelation," certainly a most marvelous production coming from the mind of an illiterate youth? He denies having been "a mere spout," as he tersely expresses it, but declares he received these " revelations" in the state of mental exaltation, his mind *en rapport* with the "entire universe."

"The history of the human mind," says Renan, "is full of strange synchronisms, by which far-distant fragments of the human race attain at the same time, without intercommunication, to ideas and imaginations almost identical. *The commerce of ideas* in the human race does not work by looks nor by direct teaching only. Jesus did not even know the name of Buddha, Zoroaster, or Plato, had read no Greek book, no Buddhist soutra; and yet there is in him more than one element which, without his knowledge, came from Buddhism, from Parseeism, or from the wisdom of the Greeks. All this is done through secret channels, and by that species of sympathy which exists between different divisions of humanity."

Some twelve years since, I occupied my leisure moments during several months with experiments in what is popularly termed *clairvoyance*. I found that by holding a lock of hair in my hand I could invariably induce the physical sensations in my own body of the person to whom the hair belonged, even when no one present knew at the time whether my description was correct or not. I frequently described features, personal appearance, and characteristics from the hair, but soon dismissed the subject as profitless, while "patients" had tongues of their own. True, I made many mistakes, but became convinced that this power did pertain to the mind. If the person to whom the hair belonged was dead, I saw the person in my mental vision only as he or she appeared when the hair was cut, and the fact of a subsequent death did not appear. Once when a dear friend was sinking into a rapid decline, I mentally obtained a botanic prescription. Of some of the ingredients, with the medical properties of which I was familiar, I gave the names; the rest I seemed to see in mental vision, as I can now call up before me the house where I was born, but their names I only ascertained by describing them as thus seen. I have no doubt whatever that the prescription saved her life: she rallied immediately, and soon regained her accustomed health. *How* this was done I cannot tell; it was not the result of will, nor were my senses closed to external things. My mental faculties were concentrated on that one point, and the "prescription" was the result.

Instances of the results of *concentration of thought* are frequent in all works treating on the philosophy of mind: it was this that enabled Mozart to compose a sonata at the age of four, and Louisa Vinning, the "Infant Sappho," to compose and sing an exquisite melody at the age of two years and eight months. "These mental concentrations can," says Dendy, "by some enthusiasts, be produced at pleasure; the paroxysm of the improvisatore, for instance. But it is an effort which, like the dark hour of the Caledonian seer, is not endured with impunity: it points, indeed, to limits beyond which mind should not be strained."

On another occasion I described a funeral which had taken place years before in the room where I was then sitting. I gave an accurate description of the grouping of the guests, the location of the remains, the position of the officiating clergyman, and various other particulars. I have thus described, *in the presence of their friends*, persons long dead, and who were utterly unknown to me, and have always retained a vivid recollection of their personal appearance. Sympathetic impression, generally loosely termed *clairvoyance*, is an admitted fact, and rests on a scientifically defined basis; but to those unacquainted with its limitations, which are many, these cases of mental impressions seem marvelous, and the credulous are easily induced to believe whatever else may be declared by the "seer." Even now, when in the presence of a sick friend, I frequently feel the symptoms in my own body, sometimes causing severe pain. One of the last locks of hair held by me in my amateur experiments was that of a person very sick with the smallpox; in my endeavors to describe the symptoms of the disease—to me unknown at the time—I became a subject of sympathetic contagion, but very fortunately had only a light attack of varioloid. I have seen a woman so sensitive that when holding a lock of hair taken from the head of a person subject to epileptic fits, she would fall on the floor herself, and the hair would have to be wrenched from her hand. Whether the lock "of hair" is any aid or not, I do not know; it may be like the metal disk which once was thought essential in "mesmerism."

A case of sympathetic contagion was published in the Boston papers, under date of Sept. 21, 1872, as a telegraphic dispatch. It was as follows:

"New York.—Two brothers, Henry and Peter Barsman, aged thirty-two and thirty-five, died of congestive chills, near Factoryville, Staten Island, this morning, within half an hour of each other. They were taken ill the same evening, had the same symptoms beforehand, and suffered the same pangs at the same time. Their physician regards this as a case of sympathetic contagion, which is so very rare in pathology that its existence as a phenomenon of disease has often been denied."

Any extended application of the principles laid down in this chapter to the phenomena offered by *mediumship* will not be necessary, as the application is too self-evident to require an argument. In many of the so-called "tests," we will find them easily falling into line with the phenomena afforded by the manifestation of mind, and evidently the result of the same causes. A story frequently cited, and recently retold by Dr. Carpenter, is that of an admirer of the poet Young, consulting his "spirit" at a "test-circle." While sitting at the table, the "intelligence" present announced himself by raps to be Edward Young. The following conversation ensued:

"Are you Young, the poet?"

"Yes."

"The author of the 'Night Thoughts'?"

"Yes."

"If you are, repeat a line of his poetry."

In response the table spelled out, by the usual alphabetical formula, these words:

"Man is not formed to question, but adore."

"Is this in the 'Night Thoughts'?" inquired the gentleman.

"No."

"Where is it?"

"Job."

This reply was very unsatisfactory to him, and he went home to ponder on it. He bought a copy of Young's poems, and found therein a poetical commentary on the book of Job which ended with that line. Greatly surprised, he hardly knew what to think. Apparently the poet had given him a line with which he was not familiar to make the "test" more convincing. A few weeks afterwards he found a volume of Young's Poems in his own library, and, on turning to the poem in question, found it with marginal marks of his own, and was thus convinced that he had read the poem before. Dr. Carpenter, in retelling this anecdote, adds these words: "I have no doubt whatever that that line had remained in his mind, that is, in the lower stratum of it; that it had been entirely forgotten by him, as even the possession of Young's Poems had been forgotten, but that it had been treasured up as it were in some dark corner of his memory, and had come up in this manner, expressing itself in the action of the table, *just as it might come up in a dream.*"

We all know that long-forgotten events frequently appear in our dreams; faces, or facts, or scenes, thus often appear on the stage of consciousness in such moments, and no superstitious wonder is felt, and yet it is really as marvelous as the phenomena exhibited as "spiritual." Dr. Carpenter, in the above-quoted sentence, has expressed no "theory" of his own, but the well-settled conviction of all physiologists.

Dr. Draper says, "In the brain of man, impressions of whatever he has seen or heard, of whatever has been made manifest to him by his other senses, nay, even the vestiges of his former thoughts, *are stored up.* These traces are most vivid at first, but by degrees they decline in force, though they probably *never completely die out.* During our waking hours, while we are perpetually receiving new impressions from things that surround us, such vestiges are overpowered and cannot attract the attention of the mind. But in the period of sleep, when external influences cease, they present themselves to our regard, and the mind, submitting to the delusion, groups them into the fantastic forms of dreams. By the use of opium and other drugs which can blunt our sensibility to passing events, these phantasms may be made to emerge."

While sitting in a "circle," we are always requested

to remain perfectly *passive*, neither seeking to exercise the will-power against "manifestations," nor too anxious to have some particular "spirit" report, or, as the father of the Davenport Brothers beautifully expresses it, "try to keep perfectly harmonic." *Mediums* tell us that a strong desire existing in the mind to hear from some particular one often seriously interferes with the "control," but that if we will remain passive the "spirits" will endeavor to satisfy us in their own way. In the anecdote given above, the announcement made, that Edward Young was present, unconsciously awoke a train of ideas in the mind of the questioner eventuating in the quotation of the line spelled out.

We know that the action of light will impress an image on the surface of inorganic objects. A familiar experiment is to lay a key, or some other object, on a sheet of white paper, and expose it for a few minutes to the action of sunlight, and then lay the paper away where it will not be disturbed. After several months, if the paper be carried into a dark place and laid on a piece of hot metal, the spectre of the key will appear. Dr. Draper says of these experiments, "In the cases of bodies more highly phosphorescent than paper, the spectres of different objects which may have been in succession laid originally upon it will, on warming, emerge in their proper order. Indeed, I believe that a shadow never falls upon a wall without leaving there a permanent trace,—a trace which might be made visible by resorting to proper processes. All kinds of photographic drawing are in their degree examples of the kind Of the moral consequences of such facts it is not my object here to speak. But if on such inorganic substances impressions may in this way be preserved, how much more likely is it that the same thing occurs in the purposely-constituted ganglion!"

If the physical forces can thus leave permanent impressions, we may well ask whether the still higher forms of force cannot also impress other than the "purposely-constituted ganglion" of the person in whose organization they first occur. Is it unreasonable to conclude that thought is communicated from one brain to another without connecting nerves? We know that physical symptoms in one may be sympathetically experienced by another. Shall we assume that a "spirit" is necessary to account for it? Mental sympathy is fully as well established a fact as any in nature; yet we are called upon to believe that it is inexplicable by physiological laws; and this request, so modest in its nature, comes from those who are the least versed in these laws.

All force is transmitted by wave-motion. Minute vibrations, communicated by various bodies to the surrounding medium, impinging upon the retinæ of the eyes, give rise to the sensation of sight, and the dimensions of these "light-waves" determine their *color;* waves of less intensity give rise to the sensation of heat. In the numerous cases cited above, *something* must have passed from the brain of one person to that of another. The term *mental impression* only describes the effect. An explanation of the method by which the communication of thought was made necessitates the existence of waves of brain-force passing from one brain to another. Prof. Gunning, in the essay already referred to, makes use of the following language: "When Dr. Bell began the investigation of spiritualism, he was surprised to find the mediums echoing back his own thoughts. He supposed that these persons had the power, in some mysterious way, of looking into our minds and seeing what is passing there. He was perplexed and baffled, and stopped the investigation, denying the intervention of spirits, but not claiming to have explained the phenomenon. Others have had the same experience. I have had it myself. Since I have begun to investigate these things, I have often found my own thoughts coming back to me from the entranced sensitive; but I soon discovered that this occurred only when I was fixing my mind more or less intently on the sensitive, and unconsciously mesmerizing her or him. I have no doubt that a great part of that which comes to us from these persons, even when they are honest and do not mean to deceive, is only the reflection of what is passing in the minds of good, fleshly, solid men and women who are present at the sittings. But I question very seriously the position of Dr. Bell, that *everything* which comes from the entranced sensitive is taken from the mind of some living person."

True, if we will use the word mind in its narrow and restricted sense. But I trust sufficient facts have been adduced to convince us that we should *expect* to meet the reflections of thoughts not present in the conscious mind, and phenomena of this class constitute the keystone to the arch with which modern delusion has attempted to span the "great gulf." Loosen this, and the whole fabric falls into the bottomless abyss of nothingness.

Before concluding this chapter it is desirable to say a few words on the mysterious power of prevision often manifested by the mind. A few cases have already been incidentally given; but others will more clearly establish the fact.

Dr. Forbes Winslow, in his work on "Obscure Diseases of the Brain and Mind," thus alludes to this singular fact in mental pathology: "Persons who have been attacked by epilepsy, paralysis, and apoplexy have had for some period previous to their seizures distinct recollection of dreaming of these affections: in fact, they seem to have *a clear presentiment* of their particular disease, as well as a prophetic inspiration of their mode of death."

In a note, Dr. Winslow quotes from a French work a number of instances which are explicable on the old theory of physiological writers, that the physical symptoms are unconsciously perceived by the mind before the conscious self has noted them. The note, presented herewith, is a quotation from the "Anatomie comparée du Système nerveux," etc., by Drs. Leuret and Gratiolet.

"In certain respects dreams ought to be attentively studied; natural instinct can in certain cases, while inciting the imagination to certain ideas, induce useful dreams, containing salutary warnings. Aspasia thus learnt the simple remedy which restored her to health; and it was likewise in a dream that the physician Abenzoar had the revelation of a medicine by the aid of which he freed himself from severe ophthalmia. If one, in fact, notices the extreme facility with which the ideas, free from the chain of exterior impressions, associate themselves during sleep, one can conceive how, in the midst of a thousand strange combinations, luminous perceptions sometimes arise. One can explain in the same way the marvelous perspicacity of certain dreamers, who, under one form or other, seem to foresee diseases of which the germ until then had been latent. Arnauld de Villeneuve dreamt one night that a black cat bit him on the side. The next day an anthrax appeared on the part bitten. A patient of Galen's dreamt that one of his limbs was changed into stone. Some days after, this leg was paralyzed. Such also was the case of the woman of whom Gunther has spoken: she dreamt that she was being beaten by a whip. In the morning she bore lesions like scars. Roger d'Oxteyn, knight of the Company of

Douglass, went to sleep in good health. Towards the middle of the night he saw in his dream a man infected with the plague, quite naked, who attacked him with fury, threw him on the ground after a desperate struggle, and, holding him between his open thighs, vomited the plague into his mouth. *Three* days after, he was seized with the plague and died."

Let us now turn to another case, narrated by a most competent authority, along with a number of remarkable dreams well worth consulting. I quote from Abercrombie's "Intellectual Powers:" "A clergyman had come to this city (Edinburgh) from a short distance in the country, and was sleeping at an inn, when he dreamed of seeing a fire, and one of his children in the midst of it. He awoke with the impression, and *instantly* left town on his return home. When he arrived within sight of his house, he found it on fire, and got there in time to assist in saving one of his children, who, in the alarm and confusion, had been left in a situation of danger."

A somewhat similar instance occurred recently in the State of Maine. An employé on a railroad in that State, one night, while asleep in another town from that in which his family resided, dreamed that the lives of the members of his family were in some impending danger. Waking with this impression on his mind, he hurriedly dressed himself, and was fortunate enough to catch a train about leaving. On his arrival home, he found the family asleep, and nearly suffocated with the gas which had escaped from the stove.

In the cases quoted by Dr. Winslow, physiology supplies us with a clue to their solution. Yet to the ignorant or unreflecting mind they are just as good "tests" of imaginary "influences" as any presented in the columns of the spirital press; and these additional instances, even if not resolvable by the same method, give us no reason to believe that a disembodied mind *must* be assumed for the occasion, with an assumed power to "impress" knowledge through that most doubtful of all avenues to knowledge, a dream!

The fact that human lives were in danger, and otherwise might have been sacrified, has nothing to do with the argument. If *presentiments* are whispered revelations, they must include the trivial as well as the important. Science can draw no distinction between impressions that lives are in danger, and those announcing the approach of a "dun" or casual callers. The lady to whom I have before referred as having frequently received mental impressions, when quite a child, exclaimed one night after ten o'clock, "Mother, Uncle George is coming!" referring to an uncle of hers who lived a dozen or more miles away in the country, where no railroad communication existed. Laughing at the girl, her mother bade her go to sleep. In the course of an hour, "Uncle George" drove up to the house and went in. His visits there were very infrequent, often a year or more intervening. Although no lives or property were at stake in this exercise of prevision by the mind of that little girl, it must take its place with the "accredited manifestations." Generous as the spiritists are with their bestowal of powers to the "invisibles," but few would ascribe this incident to a ghostly gossip.

When we take into consideration the *fact* that of the tens of thousands of impressions registered in the brain but few are present in consciousness; the *fact* that the rest exist undestroyed, and *may* be at any moment restored to consciousness; and the *fact* that thought, under certain conditions, may be communicated from one mind to another by pure volition, we may safely lay down these additional conclusions as pertaining to the unconscious brain:

IX. It can transmit thought to sensitive minds without the exercise of volition;

X. It can thus transmit thought *not* present in consciousness;

XI. It can obtain ideas, by some as yet inexplicable method, when no person is present, or which were never known to those who are present;

XII. It can "manifest" a faculty of prevision, which, often dormant, is capable of being called into action.

CHAPTER V.

"WHAT PHENOMENA OCCUR?"

1. *Liability to self-delusion.*

PHYSICAL manifestations are supposed by the spiritist to differ from the class already reviewed, in that they not only involve no action of the *medium's* mental faculties, but are confined to phenomena which may be subdivided into two classes: those in which the arms or limbs are automatically moved, and those in which physical objects are moved by unseen agencies; the *medium* constituting a reserve fund of force from which the "spirits" draw to affect grosser material. Thus, when profane hands place printer's ink on the instruments used by the "spirit-band" attending Mrs. Andrews, of Moravia notoriety, and the marks of the ink are subsequently found on her hands, or on her lips, if the trumpet was so anointed, the spiritual "law of transference" is announced, and regarded as a complete reply to the suspicions held by the "unharmonic" skeptics.

In cases of "obsession," trance, etc., the more intelligent spiritist acknowledges some undefinable relation as existing between the mental endowments of the *medium* and the intellectual characteristics of the communication or address. In what are termed physical manifestations, however, no such connection is assumed. The writing *medium*, for instance, is controlled in the arm alone, we are told, and not through the brain, if the writing be produced without the attention of the writer being directed to it. The movement of heavy bodies, the tiltings of tables and pianos, the elongation and diminution of the body, apparitions of the dead, and writing by unseen hands, are classed as *facts*, to be daily seen and subject to investigation, facts in which any conscious or unconscious action of the brain cannot be referred to for an explanation. Notwithstanding the explicitness of this claim, a more critical investigation than that generally undertaken in "harmonic circles" will tend to dissipate a large share of it, and classify much of the phenomena in question under the head of mental delusions. I have already referred at some length to the proper estimate to be placed on the evidence furnished by the senses when adduced in support of what is considered supernatural, or out of the ordinary course of experience, but desire to call attention again to some of the numerous ways in which we may be deceived even in phenomena supposed to be independent of the mind.

An experiment once in vogue, before the advent of the modern mode of explaining all acts singular and unaccountable, was to place a glass goblet on a table, and with a metallic button suspended from a string held just within it, the button would commence to oscillate and would strike the sides of the glass the number of times the holder of the string may have requested. *Investigation* soon convinced the skeptical that this result did follow, even when the request was merely a mental one. With the elbow firmly placed on the table, and the string held between the thumb and fore-finger, is made the request, and lo! the desired number is soon struck, and the button slowly regains its former motionless position. What more convincing *test* could be conceived? Beyond this there lay the possibility of obtaining letters, words, sentences, spelled out by means of the alphabet, if they had been attempted. The "investigator" felt assured that he or she had not moved a muscle of the arm, stood ready, if necessary, to make solemn attestation to it, and yet the strange result was again and again attained. Investigation of a different sort, proceeding from those whose minds were not of the "passive receptivity" school, soon discovered that while the eyes were closed or diverted the expected result did not follow. Faith was also noticed to have a marvelous effect in accelerating the motion of the mystic button; and when it was discovered that under the control of confident anticipation the arm had unconsciously swayed the cord till the desired number had been struck, the illusion was dispelled. The charm being broken, the button thenceforth stubbornly refused to move; for, the secret once known, the scarce perceptible action of the muscles was noticed and corrected.

So also it may happen in a large number of cases of table-tipping and kindred "manifestations." I say a large number of cases, for I cannot agree with Dr. Carpenter that all cases of table-tipping can be referred to this source. I believe there are "physical manifestations," neither the result of deception, conscious or unconscious, on the one hand, nor the product of imagination on the other. Their nature, and the supposed evidence of the presence of disembodied beings based on their occurrence, will be fully considered in a subsequent section.

Dr. Faraday, whose name is always mentioned with grateful reverence (except by the spiritist who has far "progressed" above the low aims of "mole-eyed science" and who obtains his scientific acquirements from the spheres), investigated the phenomenon of table-tipping, and, not having his mind in a condition of "passive receptivity," arrived at some conclusions on the subject.

He designed a simple instrument to serve as an index to the unconscious pressure exerted by those having their hands on the table. He constructed two boards, with small rollers placed between them. This was to be placed on the table, and upon it the fingers were to rest In this manner the slightest pressure of the hand could be at once noticed by the sliding of the board, and attention being thus called to the pressure, it would be at once corrected. The lack of reverence displayed in the construction of this simple indicator evidently highly displeased the "invisibles," for thenceforth they refused to honor with their presence any circle using it. I have repeatedly sat at circles formed by friends around my own sober table, who desired, "just for fun," to see if they were *mediumistic*, and have seen the table rocking back and forth or revolving round, giving no little trouble to the operators to keep their fingers on its surface; yet never, on any occasion, have I had the least reason to believe that any mental influence was involved outside of the merry group clustered around it, and often frantically endeavoring to keep up with its increasing speed, until, worn out by exhaustion, they would remove their hands, and the table would again become the staid and useful piece of furniture its maker designed. When a group of persons sit around a table, their minds filled with the dominant idea that "spirits" are present, and are in a high state of expectancy to behold something marvelous, it would be a far greater wonder if their curiosity was not satisfied to some extent than anything that could be "manifested" to them.

There are a large class of physical manifestations that are unworthy of serious attention. I allude to those produced by the itinerant jugglers who travel through the country, attempting, by means of iron rings and tin horns, so-called demonstrations of *spiritual* existence. Many of these so-called *mediums*, I am firmly convinced, are arrant cheats, having no faith in the "Gospel of the New Dispensation," but anxious only for the "scrip" to be gathered from the pockets of the credulous. The well-known *mediums* for physical manifestations, the Davenport Brothers, Laura V. Ellis, the Eddys, Mr. Reed, and last, though by no means least, the redoubtable Fay, by confining their powers to "dark circles" or "cabinet séances" can furnish us with nothing that can meet the requirements of independent investigation, because the darkness in which their feats are performed renders any critical observation impossible. These feats, we should remember, have all been duplicated by others, who made no claim to ghostly aid. These *mediums* announce themselves to their audiences as about to present some marvelous phenomena, the cause of which they leave to each to ascertain or determine as he may see fit. All of those whose names are mentioned above have passed through "exposures" again and again, as the skeptical assert, but the believers in their *mediumistic* powers continue to rely upon them as worthy of all credence.

Our liability to self-delusion is strikingly illustrated in the matter of apparitions. Thousands of persons declare that they daily see the forms of the departed, and converse with them as unmistakably as they do with their friends "still in the form." Let us examine somewhat briefly the degree of importance possessed by these undoubtedly honest declarations. In so doing, it will be well to refer to some instances not explicable upon the spiritual hypothesis, and see if they do not present many characteristics in common with more recent narratives.

Dr. Forbes Winslow relates some singular instances. "A nobleman," he says, "for some weeks previously to an attack of apoplexy, was subject to a curious phantasm. He, on several occasions during the day, when suffering from an acute headache, saw *clearly* a spectral image resembling himself. This form of hallucination is termed *deuteroscopia*. The phenomenon is considered of rare occurrence even among the insane. Aristotle refers to this type of illusion. It is explained more at length in his Metaphysics. A certain Antipheron, Aristotle says, when he was walking, saw a phantasmal reflection of himself advancing towards him. A traveler who had passed a long time without sleeping, perceived one night his own image which rode by his side. It imitated all his actions. The horseman having to cross a river, the phantom passed over it with him. Having arrived at a place where the mist was less thick, this curious apparition vanished. Goethe relates having had a similar hallucination."

Such instances as these require no explanation to intelligent readers. Yet similar instances are recorded in the spirital journals as evidences of man's immortality! In the nomenclature of spirital science they are termed "phenomena of the double," and are seriously asserted to be objective existences, thus demonstrating the existence of a "spirit" in man by its manifestations *out* of the body, leaving its tenement to thrive as best it may in the mean while. This curious phenomenon is no longer "of rare occurrence," for there exists scarcely a *medium* but can relate instances when his soul has "gone out" of the body. How often *mediums* are deprived of an indwelling soul we cannot determine, but they seem to live as well without it as when it deigns to remain. It is undoubtedly very refreshing and consolatory to some persons to know that they have souls, even if their manifestations are confined to appearances *out* of the body. So many are ready to vouch for the truth of the fact that their souls have " gone out," that we will cheerfully concede the point, and only require stronger evidence that they have ever returned.

Voices of the disembodied dead, many think, are heard the same as mortal voices; the vibrations of the air enter the ears of all men alike, but only those having a finer sense of hearing, the result of the development of the "interior" spirital sense of hearing, are aware of the fact. Dr. Winslow has some examples of this form of delusion so pertinent that I cannot refrain from again quoting from his excellent treatise:

"A worthy clergyman now under my treatment is subject to the most singular aural illusions. Several years back he had a severe attack of carbuncle at the nape of the neck. After recovering from this affection, he began to hear voices audibly speak to him. They often addressed him in the Welsh language, occasionally using particular phrases, idioms, and endearing epithets that he had been in the habit of indulging in *forty* years previously, when paying court to his wife. On one occasion he was seated by my side whilst I was occupied in writing a prescription. Appearing somewhat abstracted, I asked ' whether he then heard the voices speaking to him.' ' Yes, quite distinctly.' I said, ' What are they saying?' He rejoined, 'I would rather not repeat the words, as they are not very complimentary to yourself.' After begging him to inform me what observations these unseen spirits hovering about us were making, he replied that they were ejaculating, ' Don't leave your living; don't go abroad ; remain in England ; don't do what he recommends; don't take the medicine he prescribes.' I had endeavored to impress upon this patient's mind the importance of his relieving himself for a time from all anxious and responsible clerical and parochial duty. I advised a continental tour, with the view of trying the effect of a thorough change of air and scene, having found, in cases similar to his, much benefit from this mode of treatment. Whatever I suggested for the re-establishment of this clergyman's health, these imaginary persons did their best, most uncourteously, to oppose."

"Under the irresistible influence of an imaginary voice, many a person is driven to acts of violence and homicide. Occasionally the illusions of hearing are of a double character, that is, the patient is apparently subject to the influence of two distinct voices, a good and a bad voice,— one urging him to sacrifice life, the other a restraining voice, begging and imploring him not to yield to his dangerously insane impulses. 'My bad voices urge, my good voices restrain me,' was the remark of a patient who believed himself to be demoniacally possessed. 'I should have destroyed myself long ago,' said an insane person to Dr. Morel, 'or I should have killed somebody else, if the voice of my good angel had not begged and encouraged me to suffer.' Patients often contend with these antagonistic illusions, or 'double voices,' as Morel designates them. In one ear the most frightfully obscene ideas are suggested, whilst in the opposite one sentiments of the greatest purity will be whispered to the disordered imagination of the sufferer. These antagonistic and opposing illusions lead to fearful contests, and produce a sad amount of mental agony. 'Which voice ought I to obey?' said a delicate and sensitive-minded patient to me one day after a fit of hysterico-maniacal excitement. 'I am urged by persons that address me on my right side to utter blasphemous and indecent expressions, and to commit acts the most repulsive and repugnant to my nature; whilst in the opposite ear I clearly recognize the tender voice (conscience?) beseeching me not to yield to the fearful temptations of Satan, but to battle with his vile and wicked suggestions.'

"An insane patient was urged by an imaginary voice to destroy himself. He was commanded to cut his throat. The words *blood, blood, blood,* were repeated with terrible emphasis and in rapid succession; and on more than one occasion he was discovered with a razor, seriously contemplating self-destruction. This gentleman was subject to the influence of the double voice; for at times, when the word blood was ringing awfully in his ear, and an air-drawn dagger, stained with gore, glittered before his eyes, there stood, as he imagined, on the opposite side of his body a good spirit, whispering to him texts of Scripture, repeating verses of hymns applicable to his then state of mind, and imploring him, in most affectionate and touching language, not to eternally damn his soul by destroying his own life."*

That these are the ravings of the insane should not be objected by the spiritist. True, the delusions were of a more "progressed state of development," but these aural delusions were no more acute or convincing than those heard by our "hearing mediums." We are not to forget, moreover, that the learned "spirit-band" presiding at the Free Circle Room of the *Banner of Light* declare that a great majority of the insane are really "under control," and they would render strait-jackets useless by the adoption of the more restorative process of magnetic passes! Voices must necessarily be associated with intelligent beings, for no one would conceive an articulate voice to proceed from

---

* Dr. Forbes Winslow: "Obscure Diseases of the Mind," pp. 155, 384.

an inanimate object; but in the illusion of spectral appearance the phantom may be of any form in nature, and present all the distinguishing features of a living or of an inert body.

Sir David Brewster, in his interesting "Letters on Natural Magic," cites twelve instances of spectral illusions experienced by a lady friend,—Mrs. A. On one occasion, while engaged at her toilet before the dressing-glass, "she was suddenly startled by seeing in the mirror the figure of a near relation. The apparition appeared over her left shoulder, and its eyes met hers in the glass. It was enveloped in grave-clothes, closely pinned, as is usual with corpses, round the head and under the chin; and, though the eyes were open, the features were solid and rigid. The dress was evidently a shroud, as Mrs. A. remarked even the punctured pattern usually worked in a peculiar manner round the edges of that garment. Mrs. A. described herself as at the time sensible of a feeling like what we conceive of fascination, compelling her for a time to gaze on this melancholy apparition, which was as *distinct* and *vivid* as any reflected reality could be, the light of the candles upon the dressing-table appearing to shine fully upon its face." Truly a most "remarkable manifestation," were it not for the fact that the mortal form of her relative "was then in Scotland, and in perfect health."

On other occasions she saw apparitions of persons who were living, clad either in the habiliments of the grave or in their usual costumes. One of the first instances of illusion in her experience was the form of her husband standing in the room with his back to the fire, though he had left the house half an hour previously for a walk. Sir David says, "The apparition was seen in broad daylight, and lasted four or five minutes. When the figure stood close to her *it concealed the real objects behind it*, and the apparition was fully as vivid as the reality." Deceased friends "appeared" to her in their former dress, and seated themselves in the room; and on some occasions the ghostly form of a cat or dog would be seen in the room, or a spectral carriage-and-four would drive up the entrance-road. Fortunately Mrs. A. was a lady of intelligence, and lived before the " communion of spirits " had been reduced to an exact science.

Let us take her experience, and suppose it to occur in our own land, at the present time, to one not disinclined to believe in the spiritual philosophy. We may safely venture to say that many of the apparitions would be of a different character. Back of the spectral illusions would be a mind prepared to believe in their objective reality. This conviction would become *the dominant idea*, and unconsciously shape the appearance of the spectral forms. Instead of cats and dogs, living persons, or inanimate objects, this controlling idea would cause all such phantoms to assume the form of departed beings. Mrs. A. was convinced of the illusory nature of these phantoms, and consequently any object might appear before her disordered sight as readily as impressions are brought before the consciousness in dreams; while in the mind of the spiritist the conviction that "the departed are ever with us" would determine the character of the spectral forms.

It is not necessary to rely upon supposition alone in support of these statements. Some time since there appeared a communication in the *American Spiritualist*, in which the writer narrated a "manifestation" occurring through the well-known *medium* Charles Foster, who is said to be one of the best "physical *mediums*" in the United States. A lady visitor received a communication from the sublimated form of a brother of whom nothing had been heard for years. When last heard from, he was in the army during the rebellion, and his fate was unknown till he "appeared" to Mr. Foster and gave a circumstantial account of his capture by the Confederate soldiers, his imprisonment, and eventual death. That nothing might be wanting to present a complete "test" to his sorrowing sister, he was "seen" by Mr. Foster in his army uniform. This revelation from "the unseen shore" brought relief to an anxious heart that gladly listened to the description of the happiness now enjoyed in the brighter world above. This sweet consolation, however, was destined to be removed, for subsequently the young scapegrace returned from California!

Once thoroughly convinced of the objective reality of these illusions, no limit is to be placed to the extent to which the mind may be carried. It may pass through the stage of "development" requisite to fit its possessor for admission to Bedlam, or prepare him to accept any tale if asserted to be a "manifestation." Mundane science, through Sir David Brewster, says, "Although it is not probable that we shall ever be able to understand the actual manner in which a person *of sound mind* beholds spectral apparitions in the broad light of day, yet we may arrive at such a degree of knowledge on the subject as to satisfy rational curiosity and to strip the phenomena of every attribute of the marvelous. Even the vision of natural objects presents to us insurmountable difficulties, if we seek to understand the precise part which the mind undertakes in perceiving them; but the philosopher considers that he has given a satisfactory explanation of vision when he demonstrates that distinct pictures of external objects are painted on the retina, and that this membrane communicates with the brain by means of nerves of the same substance as itself, and of which it is merely an expansion. Here we reach the gulf which human intelligence cannot pass; and if the presumptuous mind of man shall dare to extend its speculations further, it will do it only to evince its incapacity and mortify its pride."

Spirital science, on the other hand, asserts that the gulf which yawns before the feet of the "mole-eyed" scientist *has* been bridged over by immortal intelligence, and, with the utmost contempt for *a priori* "philosophizing," makes appeal to the "facts." One of these "facts" furnished by spirital science will fully illustrate the essential difference in the methods employed by mundane and by spherical science. A few years since—in 1870, I think—an etherealized "spirit-boy" presented himself at the *Banner of Light* circle room, anxious to "communicate." What a touching picture might be drawn of the anxiety of the little fellow to again approach mortal scenes, to convince his sorrowing parents that he was still living, tenderly cared for, in a brighter world! But unfortunately for any pathetic scene that might be conjecturally assumed, the "boy" stoutly asserted that his sole object in controlling the *medium* was thereby to be endowed with the power to behold material things, as he ardently desired to visit East Boston that day to attend a circus! He chuckled exceedingly over the idea of slipping within the canvas without a ticket. Spirital science regarded this as a great "test"! "So childlike," "so natural," were some of the opinions presenting themselves to the spirital mind.

Sir Walter Scott, in concluding his "Letters on Demonology," used language that may well be quoted as strikingly applicable to our own time. He says, "Those who are disposed to look for them may, without much trouble, see such manifest signs, both of superstition and the disposition to believe in its doctrines, as may render it no useless occupation to compare the follies of our fathers with our own. The sailors have a proverb that every man in his life must eat a peck of impurity; and it seems yet more clear that every generation of the human race must swallow a certain measure of nonsense."

2. *Tendency of scientific research.*

The present century has witnessed the grandest discovery made in physical science since the time of Newton,—the discovery of the persistence and correlation of forces; a discovery now generally conceded, and possessing the most far-reaching results. That heat is not a specific entity, but rather an affection of matter, was long ago seen. Even Bacon and Locke gave some intimations of this in their works; but modern research has indubitably established the fact that heat is a "mode of motion." As a stone dropped into a pool of water transmits its motion in the ripples seen radiating in all directions on its surface, so a body dropping on a solid surface and brought to a state of rest transmits its motion to the particles of matter upon which it strikes. The molar motion expends itself by producing molecular motion; the visible motion of the whole body ceases, and the molecular motion, or motion of the particles, becomes manifest in the form of heat. All physical forces are thus shown to be convertible; that is, the expenditure of one mode of force gives rise to the manifestation of another. Repeated experiments have shown that the forces known as heat, light, electricity, and magnetism are mutually correlated, are in fact but different manifestations or modes of motion.

As in sound we have vibrations of the atmosphere striking upon the tympanum of the ear and giving rise to the sensation of hearing, so in light we have vibrations of an all-pervading ether impinging upon the retina of the eye and causing the sensation known as sight. Nor has the discovery ended with the correlation of the physical forces, for investigations conducted by Mayer, Carpenter, Le Conte, and others, demonstrated that the so-called vital forces were but modes of manifestation of the same force, or, as Dr. Carpenter has expressed it, "that so clear a mutual relationship exists between all the vital forces that they might be legitimately regarded as modes of one and the same force."

Herbert Spencer asserts that all *a priori* possibilities and experimental evidence alike warrant us in the belief "that there cannot be an *isolated force* beginning and ending in nothing; but that any force manifested implies an equal antecedent force from which it is derived and against which it is a reaction. Further, that the force so originating cannot disappear without result, but must expend itself in some other manifestation of force, which, in being produced, becomes its reaction, and so on continually."—*First Principles*. In another work ("Principles of Biology," i. p. 57) he states, "It is a corollary from that primordial truth which, as we have seen, underlies all other truths, that whatever amount of power an organism expends in any shape is the correlate and equivalent of a power that was taken into it from without. On the one hand it follows from the persistence of force that each portion of mechanical or other energy which an organism exerts implies the transformation of as much organic matter as contained this energy in a latent state. And on the other hand it follows from the persistence of force that no such transformation of organic matter containing this latent energy can take place without the energy being in one shape or other manifested."

Contractility is the essential attribute of the muscle, and is peculiarly a vital endowment, yet it can be excited, for a time, after death, when the "vital principle" is supposed to have left the body. During life this movement of the muscles is the result of a stimulus transmitted by the nerves. Mr. G. H. Lewes has shown, and subsequent research has abundantly verified it, that there is no real difference in property between the sensory and motor nerves. Dr. Bastian, in his recent work on "The Beginnings of Life," remarks, "Neurility is the characteristic property of a nerve, just as contractility is the characteristic property of a muscle; and the different results produced when a sensory and motor nerve respectively are stimulated are due to the different nature of the organs to which the stimulus is directed. When the stimulus traverses the nerve in an *afferent* direction, this, impinging upon a nerve-centre, liberates a larger or smaller quantity of energy, and may produce what is called a sensation; but when, on the other hand, a stimulus originating in a nerve-centre is propagated in an *efferent* direction, then this stimulus calls into play the contractility of a muscle, and so gives rise to a motor act."

I have recalled these established principles of scientific research to the reader's attention, because the whole theory of spirital physical manifestations is in direct conflict with them. The spiritist still regards all the phenomena of life as the *direct* result of a mysterious entity, an "etherealized and sublimated" being dwelling within the body during physical life and using the body as a machine for its own use; while modern thought, forming its conclusions from the study of organic forms, regards life as an abstract term, signifying the properties exhibited by what are termed living bodies to distinguish them from those not manifesting these properties. Modern research endeavors to understand the relation existing between the manifestation of thought and the forces *employed* in keeping the thinking apparatus in perfect tune. The metaphysical idea of life being a specific entity was the direct cause of the ready belief accorded to the tales of earlier days of transformations of persons into animals, as narrated in witchcraft prosecutions. This philosophy may be found more fully elaborated in some of the tales in the Arabian Nights' Entertainment.

While looking upon the phenomena of life as the peculiar field of physical research, modern thought is met by the bold assumption that its method of investigation will necessarily rob the soul of all hopes of the future, blot out the divine spark of immortal life, and leave us with only a visible horizon to bound our powers. This assertion has been so many times and so fully met by abler hands, that we need not be deterred in our purpose by having it again flaunted in our way. We know that we are physical beings; we inhabit a physical world, and in structural form have many points of resemblance to inferior forms of life. Intelligence in man, as in many of these inferior forms, is manifested by much the same processes. The mechanism of thought is a legitimate study for science. Even if our conclusions should be antagonistic to many of our former metaphysical notions, it does not necessarily follow that they must be false. The bugbear of "atheistic materialism" need not frighten us, even if science should confirm the views of Dr. Bastian, that "cognition or intellectual action may take place under the form of a mere *organic* or *un-*

conscious discrimination, without the intervention of consciousness. Thus, in the individual, consciousness or feeling comes to be superadded as an additional accompaniment to certain mere organic discriminations; so that consciousness, without which sensation cannot exist, is secondary, whilst cognition, in the form of unconscious discrimination, is primary. Out of this primary undifferentiated organic discrimination, such as alone pertains to the lowest forms of animal life, there has been gradually evolved that which we know as feeling and consciousness."

Those who are still determined to discover evidence of spiritual realities in the domain of physical science may well be alarmed at the conflict physical science is bringing on. The two lines of thought, so far from being antagonistic, are in parallel directions, and neither approach nor recede from each other. Whatever may be the result of the inquiry into the genesis of mind will in no degree pronounce an ultimate decision on the question of its destiny. However intimate a relation may be shown to subsist between mental processes and the expenditure of force, we are still to bear in mind that " the intellectual product does not belong to the category of forces at all. It does not answer their definition as 'that which is expended in producing or resisting motion.' It is not reconvertible into other forms of force. One cannot lift a weight with a logical demonstration, nor make a tea-kettle boil by writing an ode to it. A given amount of molecular action in two brains represents a certain equivalent of food, but by no means an equivalent of intellectual product. . . . . We must not forget that force-equivalent is one thing, and quality of force-product is quite a different thing. The same outlay of muscular exertion turns the winch of a coffee-mill and of a hand-organ. I am not sure that mental qualities are not as susceptible of measurement as the aurora borealis or the changes of the weather. But even measurable *quality* has no more to do with the correlation of forces than the color of a horse with his power of draught; and it is with quality we more especially deal in intellect and morals." *

The spiritists are the most notable of modern opponents of scientific thought, inasmuch as they are unable to realize the changes which have taken place in the world of thought during the present century. They still cling to the scholastic error that soul and life are in some mysterious manner identical, and seek to interpret physical phenomena in such a manner as to understand in physical terms the mechanism of spirit! These crude attempts at interpreting phenomena as "physical manifestations" of spiritual life are in direct conflict with philosophy and science, and the reasons often so ostentatiously set forth by this school may be described, in the words of Herbert Spencer, as "those vitiations of evidence due to random observations, to the subjective states of the observers, to their enthusiasms, or prepossessions, or self-interests; those that arise from the general tendency to set down as a fact observed what is really an inference from an observation, and also those that arise from the general tendency to omit the dissection by which small surface-results are traced to large interior causes."

In treating of the tendency of modern thought, it may be well to see in what manner some of the most painstaking investigators have met the objection of "materialism," so often urged to-day, as well as in the past. Claude Bernard, Professor of Physiology in the College of France, has seen fit to refer to this charge. He says,—

---

* Oliver Wendell Holmes: "Mechanism in Thought and Morals," pp. 64, 67.

"Preconceived ideas clearly have a great influence in discussing the functions of the brain, and a solution is combated by arguments used for the sake of their tendency. Some refuse to allow that the brain can be the organ of intelligence, from fear of being involved by that admission in materialistic doctrines; while others eagerly and arbitrarily lodge intelligence in a round or fusiform nerve-cell, for fear of being charged with spiritualism. For ourselves, we are not concerned about such fears. Physiology tells us that, except in the difference and greater complexity of the phenomena, the brain is the organ of intelligence in exactly the same way that the heart is the organ of circulation and the larynx that of the voice. We discover everywhere a necessary bond between the organs and their functions; it is a general principle, from which no organ of the body can escape. Physiology should copy the example of more advanced sciences, and free itself from the fetters of philosophy that would impede its progress; its mission is to seek truth calmly and confidently, its object is to establish it beyond doubt or change, without any alarm as to the form under which it may make its appearance."

That the brain, or the whole nervous system, is the organ of mind, is a conclusion in no way fraught with the terrible results so many imagine. Dr. Carpenter has spent a lifetime investigating the physiology of mind, and on more than one occasion has expressed his belief in terms no one can regard as materialistic. He is of the opinion "that science points to (though at present I should be far from saying that it demonstrates) the origination of all power in mind. . . . When metaphysicians, shaking off the bugbear of materialism, will honestly and courageously study the phenomena of the mind of man in their relation to those of his body, I believe that they will find in their relation their best arguments for the presence of infinite mind in universal nature."

Modern science has swung clear from its old moorings, and is rapidly seeking to embrace all phenomena within its domain. Mind can no longer claim to be beyond its grasp and to dwell secluded in mystery. The tendency of thought in this direction is forcibly expressed by a recent writer, as follows : "Whilst the manifestation of mental phenomena, in the ordinary sense of the term, corresponds only to a fractional part of nerve-activities in general, there is, again, the very best reason for believing that consciousness, so far from being coextensive with mind, or mental phenomena, is in reality *limited to a comparatively small portion* of what may be rightly ranged under this category. Many truly mental phenomena never reveal themselves in consciousness at all, and the roots of these strike far and wide : so that, instead of accepting the popular view that the brain is the organ of mind, I believe it would be nearer the truth to look upon the whole nervous system as the organ of mind,—a doctrine which has already been taught by Mr. G. H. Lewes and others. The brain, it is true, is its principal organ, whilst consciousness or feeling is probably only attendant upon the activity of quite a limited portion of this. And, as Mr. Herbert Spencer has so clearly pointed out, in the evolution of mind we each one of us experience the constant transitions whereby a state or act (the recurrence of which was at first always attended by consciousness) at last, when thoroughly familiar, *may take place quite unconsciously*, or without in the least arousing our attention. The more fully such phenomena, therefore, are recognized as parts of an orderly succession, by which alone greater and greater complexities of thought and feeling are rendered possible, the more will it become evident that the sphere of mind cannot at any time be circumscribed by the then present or possible states of consciousness,—the more it is obvious that in our conception of mind we should also include *all past stages of consciousness*, the representatives of which, now in the form of unconscious nerve-actions, are from moment to moment manifesting themselves potentially, if not actually, in all our present thoughts, feelings, and volitions."*

An able article some time since appeared in the *Popular Science Review* (London), contributed by Dr. Richardson, in which he contends that the nerves are enveloped in a nerve-fluid or ether, that by its molecular motion sensation is communicated and the commands of the will transmitted. He states that it extends in all persons more or less *beyond* the extremities of the nerve-structure, varying in depth and density in various persons. Mr. Crookes, F.R.S., the editor of the *Quarterly Journal of Science* and of the *Chemical News*, more widely known by reason of his investigations of the *mediumship* of Mr. D. D. Home, has constructed an instrument of extreme delicacy, which seems to indicate the existence of such a "nerve-atmosphere" as more or less encompassing every person with whom he has made trial of it.

Many of the phenomena narrated in the preceding pages would seem to be explicable only upon the hypothesis of the existence of such a medium, in which the conscious or unconscious exercise of the mental faculties excites molecular motion, as the physical force of light excites molecular motion in the ether-filling space. In the hands of so experienced an investigator as Mr. Crookes, there is but little fear of imitating

---

* H. Charlton Bastian, M.A., M.D., F.R.S.: "The Beginnings of Life," pp. 42-44.

the fallacious methods pursued by Reichenbach in his so-called discovery of odic force, now known to be destitute of any plausible evidence. Granting the existence of such a medium as Dr. Richardson claims to have discovered, the manifestation of intelligence in spiritual phenomena would cease to be a source of wonder. Physiologists are familiar with speculations concerning the existence of a medium for the transmission of thought, which has been often broached under the names of "vital force," "brain-waves," "soul-force," or "nerve-ether;" and, although the writer is convinced that these terms shadow forth a great truth, and that Dr. Richardson's discovery will in the main be substantiated, it is not necessary to the line of argument herein pursued to devote any space to the consideration of it, or to rely upon it as an essential condition.

If I have succeeded in presenting sufficient grounds for believing that the mental phenomena are directly dependent upon the mental organization of the "*medium,*" and consequently are wholly within the domain of physiological investigation, the more detailed explanation of the methods by which they are evolved may well be left to other hands. That the unconscious brain can perform all the mental acts that are possible under the control of conscious volition has already been shown, as well as its power to exert a mental force affecting the consciousness of others; and the discovery of a "nerve-ether" would render such acts more intelligible, as well as afford an explanation of many "physical manifestations," such as the movement of heavy bodies without personal contact. That a force proceeding from the human organism can move ponderable bodies without physical contact may be a conclusion more difficult to win assent to; and yet I think it is one that can be abundantly verified.

CHAPTER VI.

PHYSICAL MANIFESTATIONS.

1. *Involuntary actions.*

"WHAT thought is," says G. H. Lewes, "we do not know, perhaps we never shall. We do not know what life is. But the realm of mystery may be reduced to one of 'orderly mystery;' we may learn what are the laws of Life, and what are the laws of Thought." So in investigating so-called physical phenomena we may be enabled to learn some of their laws, and, while frankly admitting the existence of much still mysterious, may still feel convinced that the phenomena *cannot* be the effect of invisible personal agents, and that the mystery can be shown to lie in our failure to comprehend the natural processes involved. In a previous chapter it has been shown that the mind, while controlled by an unconscious idea, often directs the movements of the body; that painting, reading, or writing may be performed without the fact being known to consciousness. We have seen that during abstraction, in natural sleep, and in the trance state, the connection between the brain and nerves being closed, the activity of the cerebrum is carried on independently of the sensorium, from the stock of sense-impressions stored up by memory. Attention also has been called to the fact that when the mind is "under control" by a *dominant idea*, this will invariably shape the action evolved. Dryden has said,—

"Sometimes forgotten things, long cast behind,
Rush forward in the brain, and come to mind;

> The nurse's legends are for truth received,
> And the man dreams but what the boy believed;
> Sometimes we but rehearse a former play,
> The night restores our actions done by day."

Spirital investigators are required to exhibit a *passive* frame of mind, to patiently wait for the expected manifestations. Singing is generally resorted to, that all minds may be rendered more "harmonious," as the "influences" are often seriously retarded by the action of the "will-powers" of non-passive investigators. Circles are formed which often continue for ten, twenty, or thirty nights before any phenomena are vouchsafed. A lady *medium*, well known as a "spirit-artist," sat in a circle certain evenings consecutively for months before she was "controlled." In this case the "spirits" had promised to develop her as an artist before the close of the year; and during the last days of December, when expectancy was at its highest point, the materials were called for and a sketch made, the lady all the while being in an unconscious trance state. This lady in her childhood, her mother once informed me, had shown a natural taste for drawing, frequently having used the juice of the elderberry for ornamental purposes on fences and barns. In her unconscious state, the *dominant idea* of "spirit-possession" and concentrated expectation assumed "control," and manifestations ensued.

In circles the great prerequisite "condition" for the successful invocation of "spirits" is recognized to be the entire passivity of the voluntary powers. "Passive receptivity" is the key to spirital favor. Each subsequent sitting confirms this use of the physical organs, until they become automatic, fixed by habit as well in this state as in the conscious moments. When Charles XII. was struck dead by a cannon-ball, he clasped his hand on the hilt of his sword. The mind requires but one-tenth of a second to form a conclusion and act accordingly, but the velocity of the ball far exceeded the "rapidity of thought," and we are thus compelled to regard the movement of the arm and hand as an unconscious reflex action. Some experiments performed on the body of a negro criminal, hanged in the city of Richmond, Va., gave an interesting illustration of the reflex action of the nerves and muscles. Under electrical stimulus the arms assumed the position necessary for playing the banjo! This was a position that had once required the constant attention of consciousness, but *habitual* use had rendered it automatic, and the voluntary power had passed into an involuntary one, capable of being induced after consciousness had forever quitted its home.

It should be borne in mind that physiology gives us no warrant for drawing a sharp line of demarcation between the voluntary and involuntary powers of the nerves. Some even assert that there exists no involuntary action but can be controlled or modified by conscious volition. Mr. G. H. Lewes, in his "Physiology of Common Life," says,—

"It is an error to assert, as most physiologists and psychologists persist in asserting, that these actions *cannot* be controlled, that they are altogether beyond the interference of other centres, and cannot by any effort of ours be modified. It is an error to suppose these actions are essentially distinguished from the voluntary movement of the hands. We have acquired a power of definite direction in the movement of the hands, which renders them obedient to our will; but this acquisition has been of slow, laborious growth. If we were asked to use our toes as we do our fingers, to grasp, paint, sew, or write with them, we should find it not less impossible to control the movement of the toes in these directions, than to contract the iris, or cause a burst of perspiration to break forth.* Certain movements of the toes are possible to us; but, unless the loss of our fingers had made it necessary that we should use our toes in complicated and slowly-acquired movements, we can do no more with them than the young infant can do with his fingers. Yet men and women have written, sewed, and painted with their toes. All that is required is that certain links should be established between sensations and movements; by continual practice these links *are* established; and what is impossible to the majority of men becomes easy to the individual who has acquired this power. This same power can be acquired over what are called the organic actions; although the habitual needs of life do not tend towards such acquisition, and without some strong current setting in that direction, or some *peculiarity of organization rendering it easy*, it is not acquired. In ordinary experience the number of those who can write with their toes is extremely rare, the urgent necessity which would create such a power being rare; and rare also are the examples of those who have any control over the movement of the iris, or action of a gland; but both rarities exist.

"It would be difficult to choose a more striking example of reflex action than the contraction of the iris of the eye under the stimulus of light, and to ordinary men, having no link established which would guide them, it is utterly impossible to close the iris by an effort. It would be not less impossible to the hungry child to get on a chair and reach the food on the table, until that child had

---

* It might seem, *a priori*, equally difficult to "cause a burst of inspiration to break forth;" yet thousands fondly believe it to be as easy of accomplishment as drawing water from a faucet.

learned how to do so. Yet there are men who have learned how to contract the iris. The celebrated Fontana had this power; which is possessed also by a medical man now living at Kilmarnock,—Dr. Paxton,—a fact authenticated by no less a person than Dr. Allen Thomson. Dr. Paxton can contract or expand the iris at will, without changing the position of his eye, and without an effort of adaptation to distance.

"To move the ears is impossible to most men. Yet some do it with ease, and all can learn to do so. Some men have learned to 'ruminate' their food; others to vomit with ease; and some are said to have the power of perspiring at will. That many glands are under the influence of the will—in other words, that we can stimulate them to secretion by a mere ideal stimulus—is too well known to need instance here. Even the beating of the heart can be arrested.

" . . . . It thus appears that even the actions which most distinctly bear the character recognized as involuntary—uncontrollable—are only so because the ordinary processes of life furnish no necessity for their control. And while it appears that the involuntary can become voluntary, it is familiar to all that the voluntary actions *tend, by constant repetition, to become involuntary*, and are then called secondary automatic."

Dendy ("Philosophy of Mystery," pp. 370-71) relates a number of instances of the power of the will over involuntary muscles; one of the suspension of the action both of the heart and lungs, during which there was no apparent vapor on the mirror held to the mouth. Of this instance he says, "During the many hours in which this voluntary trance existed, there was a total absence of consciousness, yet a faculty of *self-reanimation!*"

These examples are far more marvelous than anything

recorded of "automatic mediums." For it is more difficult for the will to direct an involuntary action, than it is for the unconscious brain, or, if the term may be used, the extra-conscious mind, when influenced by concentrated expectancy. The manifestation of intelligence, as we have seen, would, so far from being surprising, be the result naturally expected to be associated with the phenomenon. The dominant state of expectancy for the occurrence of phenomena proceeding from intelligent beings would not only operate upon the involuntary nerves with a force equal to that of conscious volition, but, it is not too much to assert, would sensibly augment the power, becoming more *concentrated* than in our conscious moments, when the mind is open to sense-impressions; and the systematic "development" of this power, at first often so laborious and protracted, on each recurring manifestation becomes more and more of the character of a "reflex action." Thus a "well-developed medium" has but to close her eyes, resign herself to *passivity*, and in a minute the hand is controlled to write, or paint. There is one point which still remains a "marvel;" that is, *how* the sense of *seeing* is exercised while the eyes are closed; but it is a "marvel" no greater than many exhibited by the somnambule and dreamer. In fact, the true solution of the phenomena, instead of being sought in the domain of "spiritual faculties" or "intuition," might be attained by a closer study of the manifestations of *instinct* in the lower forms of life, many of which are as marvelous as, *if not analogous* to, the manifestations of "soul-perceptions" in man. To all true students of nature, however, it must ever remain by far the greatest "manifestation" of this phenomena-loving age, that thousands of individuals, having attained the years of legal majority, can be found willing and even anxious to abnegate the powers of the will and become mere instruments for the manifestation of involuntary powers. To all such who may have read this work as far as the present point, the following remarks of Dr. Carpenter, quoted from "Human Physiology," are seriously commended. He says,—

"It is, in fact, the virtue of the will that we are *not* mere thinking automata, mere puppets to be pulled by suggesting strings, capable of being played upon by every one who shall have made himself master of our springs of action. It may be freely admitted that such thinking automata *do* exist; for there are many individuals whose will has never been called into due exercise, and who gradually or almost entirely lose the power of exerting it, becoming the mere creatures of habit and impulse; and there are others in whom such states are of occasional occurrence; whilst in others, again, they may be artificially induced.

"It may be unhesitatingly laid down that, if the directing powers of the will be suspended, the capability of correcting even the most illusory ideas by an appeal to 'common sense' is for the time annihilated. Of this we have a typical example in the state of dreaming. Hence we see that if the human mind should lose for a time the power of volitional self-direction it cannot shake off the yoke of any 'dominant idea,' however tyrannical, but must execute its behests;—it cannot bring any notion with which it may be possessed to the test of 'common sense,' but *must* accept it as a belief, if it be impressed on the consciousness with adequate force;—it cannot recall any fact, even the most familiar, that is beyond its immediate grasp;—upon any idea, therefore, with which it may be possessed, the whole force of its attention is for the time concentrated, so that the most incongruous conception presents itself with all the vividness of reality."

Professor Dods, in his Lectures on "Spirit Manifestations," says, "I know a Quaker lady in Salem, Mass., who, from long habits of passivity, waiting for the moving of the spirit, could strike every joint of her body together so as to be heard in an adjoining room. Nor was it in her power to prevent it. Her manner of devotion had become itself a disease. The habit was stamped upon her involuntary powers, and they ruled. She was unceasingly rapping during her waking moments, and was still only when she was asleep. She was the greatest rapping medium I ever knew." Many instances of habits voluntarily formed becoming involuntary must be familiar to all thoughtful readers, and history furnishes us with numerous cases of their having become epidemic and afflicting a whole community with "accredited manifestations." Dr. Babbington says, "The imaginations of women are always more excitable than those of men, and are therefore susceptible of every folly when they lead a life of strict seclusion and their thoughts are constantly turned inward upon themselves. Hence, in orphan asylums, hospitals, and convents, the nervous disorder of one female so easily and quickly becomes the disorder of all. A nun in a very large convent in France, by some strange impulse, began to mew like a cat. Shortly after, other nuns also mewed together every day at a certain time for several hours in succession, annoying the whole neighborhood with a cat-concert. This it was not in their power to prevent till they were relieved by a superior impression. . . . But of all the epidemics of females which I myself have seen in Germany, or of which the history is known to me, the most remarkable is the celebrated convent epidemic of the fifteenth century, which Cardan describes. A certain nun in Germany fell to biting all her companions. In the course of a short time all the nuns of this convent began biting each other. The news of this infatuation among the nuns soon spread, and passed from convent to convent through a great part of Germany, principally Saxony and Brandenburg. It afterwards visited the nunneries in Holland, and at last the nuns had the biting mania even as far as Rome."

Perhaps one of the most singular instances recorded of this nature—the contagious effect of involuntary actions—is narrated by Dr. Stone, in his work on the "Progress of Fanaticism." He is describing an extensive religious excitement in the State of Kentucky in the early part of the present century. The preacher had been a great hunter, and in his public addresses used as figures of speech words and phrases from the hunter's vocabulary. His hearers were vehemently exhorted to chase the devil and tree him as they would any wild beast endangering their households. One individual, at a grove meeting, of a sufficiently nervous temperament to be easily impressed, started off on full run in pursuit of the devil! Others were involuntarily led to join in the pursuit. Professor Dods, who investigated this statement, and saw and conversed with an eye-witness of this strange scene, says this was called "the running exercise!" Professor Dods says, "One climbed up into a tree after the devil, and others involuntarily caught the mania. This was called 'the climbing exercise!' One individual was moved to bark; and soon others, even though they used every method to prevent it, fell to involuntary barking like dogs, while others gathered around the tree praying for success. This was called 'treeing the devil!' It was literally a devil-chase! And such a time of running, climbing, dog-barking, and devil-chasing, was perhaps never known before nor since. I doubt whether it can be surpassed in any of its mysteries, even by the rapping, writing, and table-tipping business of the present day.

"On another occasion, insisting upon the words of our Saviour being literally understood,—'Except ye be converted and become as little children, ye cannot enter into the kingdom of heaven,'—one individual went to playing marbles in the broad aisle of the church; others involuntarily joined him. An old man undertook to expostulate, saying that it was carrying matters, as he thought, rather too far. On hearing this, an old lady who was down upon her knees among the marble-players sprang to her feet, grasped her umbrella, and, taking a side-saddle seat on it, rode down the aisle in full childlike glee. On seeing this, the old gentleman could resist no longer,—seized his cane, threw himself astride of it, like any boy, and rode down the aisle after her, exclaiming, in a sing-song voice, 'Oh, my dear brethren and sisters, I feel the full childlike spirit carrying me to heaven on a wooden hoss!' Several others now caught the mania, having no power to resist it. Others, less serious, broke out in convulsive laughter, shouted and hurrahed, and the meeting broke up in one scene of confusion. It was not in the power of these persons to resist it. The involuntary powers, *by one single impression*, took the entire and irresistible control."

The professor narrates another instance, referred to by Dr. Stone, the facts of which were gathered by him during his travels in North Carolina in 1832. As his book is now out of print, I shall quote the passage entire:

"A man had set himself up as a preacher who had received a commission direct from heaven, and as clergymen were not willing to admit him into their pulpits, he traveled about, preaching in groves in various sections of the State. He was a man of a very nervous temperament, and when he became excited in speaking his gestures were violent, yet impressive. Still, they were made by his voluntary powers. He possessed, also, a good faculty for expressing the various passions and emotions of the soul in his countenance, according to the sentiment he was uttering. These gestures of his hands and motions of his face, and even feet, would involuntarily continue for some time after he took his seat, while the concluding hymn was being sung, and frequently commence before he rose to speak, and, indeed, at any time when he was excited. But as he, in all these cases, exerted his voluntary powers to keep his hands, face, and feet still, so the conflict between the voluntary and involuntary powers produced, not gestures, but most violent, sudden, and irregular jerkings and twitchings. And instead of expressing the passions of his soul in his countenance, he made up the most horrible faces that can be well conceived. As he could not account for these things in himself, and as it was not in his power to prevent them, so he attributed the whole to the power of the spirit!

"Now, it so happened that every one of his converts was at first seized with these most singular spasmodic motions of the limbs and contortions of the countenance. Hence these involuntary motions were called 'the jerks,' and whenever any one was converted it was expressed by saying that such a one had got the jerks! The news of these most singular manifestations spread over the whole region round about. Persons came from a distance of twenty and even thirty miles to hear him and see the wonders. And it so happened, at length, that as many of those who came laughing and mocking were seized with the jerks as of those who were in reality converted. This was pronounced by the eccentric speaker as the curse of God upon those who scoffed. But the mania spread, exciting the mirth and ridicule of some, and the astonishment and awe of others, till the excitement became general; and such a time of jerking, twitching, and making up wry faces at each other, it is difficult to imagine, or even describe. Here, then, is a striking proof of the fact that the involuntary powers of some can be made to act suddenly, even by one solitary impression made upon the mind."

Those of my readers who have had opportunities for observing the actions of *trance-mediums* during the earlier portion of their "development" cannot have failed to notice the nervous twitchings and "jerks" that preceded the control of the involuntary powers of the mind. During the "planchette" mania I procured one of those mysterious instruments and carried it home, to see if any of my family could write with it. In the hands of one member it moved off rapidly and wrote quite distinctly, answering questions readily enough, but with very little regard to veracity if the questions were such as the person using it could not have answered herself. One of the first "communications" received was the spirital autograph of Silas Wright. In response to the suggestion that we were ready to hear anything he might see fit to communicate, the pencil wrote this sentence: "I am an honest man." No one seeming inclined to dispute the statement, we heard no more from the ex-Governor. One noticeable fact I observed in connection with this planchette writing: the lady's hand on the board, *after* repeated experiments, was seized with a spasmodic trembling, and moved off from the planchette on to the table. In response to a suggestion that "they" might desire to write by means of her hand, a pencil was furnished, and several sheets of paper were filled with illegible zigzag marks. I found that whenever she sat down with a pencil in her hand the arm would again exhibit the usual premonitory twitchings before the pencil began its markings. Once, when her mind was on a dear friend, then recently deceased, the friend's name was legibly written on the paper before her. Lack of faith, however, on her part, prevented the spirital hypothesis from becoming the dominant idea, and no other intelligible writing was produced by her hand except that given by the mendacious planchette. In those cases, however, she averred that the answers were always present in her consciousness before the pencil had finished writing, although she was unconscious of any effort on her part to influence the writing or direct the movement of the board. When a question was asked, her mind *necessarily* would form some answer, and, although volition had no conscious direction, that answer would be involuntarily written through the agency of the planchette. I have no doubt but there have been many instances where the answers were written when this connection between the working of the mind and the consciousness did not exist, and the answer would then only be known to the passive operator by seeing it written out on the paper. A firm belief in the reality of the communication would necessarily tend to produce this result. In some instances names were written entirely unknown save to some one present —one that of a school-mate of a gentleman present, long since dead, and remembered only as a school companion in earlier years. Sometimes a short "communication" would follow; other times the "control would be changed," as our friends would say, and some other idea would direct the pencil. Those who have never seen writing by this instrument, or are unable to write with it, may easily obtain similar "communications" in a far easier manner. Let one of the party be selected, who shall answer every question put, of whatever nature, on the spur of the moment, without any hesitancy or deliberation, giving the first thoughts which arise in the mind. True, there would be no *mystery* connected with it, to give a zest to the farce; but so far as the "intelligent influence" is concerned, the answers would be of the same nature as those produced through the planchette by the action of the involuntary nerves.

There are still other actions, partaking largely of the marvelous, which seem to come under a different classification from any yet considered. A few instances on record may be referred to, in order that the nature of the phenomena may be more clearly defined. Many years since, there was reported in *Silliman's Journal* a case of a lady becoming charged with electricity to such a degree that she emitted electric sparks from her fingers and toes, sometimes *seen*, *heard*, and *felt*, while at other times the sparks were neither seen nor felt, but *heard*, producing a "mysterious series of raps." The narrative says, "On the evening of January 28, during a somewhat extraordinary display of the Northern Lights, a respectable lady became so highly charged with electricity as to give out vivid electrical sparks from the end of each finger to the face of each of the company present. This did not cease with the heavenly phenomenon, but continued several months, during which time she was constantly charged and giving off electrical sparks to every conductor she approached. This was extremely vexatious, as she could not touch the stove, or any metallic utensil, without first giving off an electrical spark, with the consequent twinge. The state most favorable to this phenomenon was an atmosphere of about eighty degrees, moderate exercise, and social enjoyment. It disappeared in an atmosphere approaching zero, and under the debilitating effects of fear. When seated by the stove, reading, with her feet upon the fender, she gave sparks at the rate of three or four a minute; and under the most favorable circumstances a spark that could be seen, heard, or felt passed every second. She could charge others in the same way when insulated, who could then give sparks to others. To make it satisfactory that her dress did not produce it, it was changed to cotton and woolen, without altering the phenomenon. The lady is about thirty, of sedentary pursuits and delicate state of health, having for two years previously suffered from acute rheumatism and neuralgic affections, with peculiar symptoms."

A case somewhat more widely known was that of the French peasant-girl Angélique Cottin, in the year 1846. The first *manifestations* observed were unaccountable movements of the frame of a loom at which she was weaving silk gloves. Terrified at the apparently causeless motion, she ran to a distance, when it ceased. On again approaching the loom it recommenced its tippings. Her parents, much distressed, took the girl to the church to have the demoniacal "influence" exorcised; but the curate, fortunately being a man of sense, sent her to a physician. This singular phenomenon soon grew more marked in its manifestations, as we should naturally expect. For the girl, firmly convinced that her conscious self was not the author of these mysterious movements, would naturally think, as her parents thought, that they were the result of some "outside influence," and her mind under this impression would sink into a state of complete *passivity*, thus unconsciously aiding "development." Wherever she went the furniture moved, and articles touched by her clothes would fly as if hurled by a human hand direct from the "spheres." A man seated on a tub near which she was standing was lifted on his seat into the air. When placed on certain non-conductors of electricity these effects were observed to diminish, and insulation was at times necessary to enable her to take repose.

A somewhat similar case occurred a few years since, near Boston. An Irish servant-girl became possessed with an unaccountable attraction, by which furniture and other articles would be drawn towards her, and crockery broken without personal contact. The spirital neighbors of the family with whom the girl resided kindly offered their services to ascertain the *wishes of the "spirits"* operating through her, but their services were declined. The girl was removed to a hospital, and subsequently died, and her death was referred to by the *Banner of Light* as evidence of the injurious effects of scientific treatment, whereas, if she had been properly "developed," submitted to harmonious influences,—and so on, *ad infinitum, ad nauseam!*

In the case of the Seeress of Prevorst, Madame Hauffé, similar movements of physical objects occurred. William Howitt says, "While Madame Hauffé was spending some time at Kerner's house, gravel and ashes were thrown about where no visible creature was to throw them. A stool rose *gradually* to the ceiling and then came down again. . . . It was a fact that when Madame Hauffé was in a particularly magnetic state *she could not sink in her bath*, but rose to the surface, and could only be held down by hands." Justinus Kerner published a narrative of her eventful life, from which I make one extract: "As I had been told by her parents, a year before her father's death, that at the period of her early magnetic state she was able to make herself heard by her friends as they lay in bed at night in the same village, but in other houses, by a knocking, as is said of the dead, I asked her whether she was able to do so *now*, and at what *distance*. She answered that she would sometimes do it,—that to the spirit space was nothing. Some time after this, as we were going to bed,

—my children and servants being already asleep,—we heard a knocking as if in the air over our heads. There were six knocks, at intervals of half a minute. It was a hollow yet clear sound, soft, but distinct. On the following evening, when she was asleep, when we had mentioned the knocking to nobody whatever, she asked me whether she should soon knock to us again, which, as she said *it was hurtful to her*, I declined."

Although the "seeress" professed to *see* "spirits," no claim was ever made of their acting *through* her; she professed to act by her own power, though in what manner these electro-magnetic discharges were made audible at so great a distance is not so clear. I often make magnetic passes over persons suffering from headaches or other nervous disorders, almost invariably with complete success, and I am often assured by skeptical *patients* that they *feel* something striking on their faces or hands. Some describe it as "sparks," others as "drops of warm water." For a long time I ascribed this to imagination; but I have been assured of the same fact by gentlemen of culture, who were at first entirely skeptical of any tranquilizing effects following the "passes." Whether this feeling be founded on fact or imagination, I never was conscious of being a *medium* in allaying nervous disorders, although I have met with perfect success with friends who were *at the time* delirious.

In *Appletons' Journal* for November 12, 1870, is an interesting article on Electrical Persons and Places, by H. Butterworth. The author refers to some of the instances narrated above, and gives others equally remarkable. I will quote one or two instances:

"A careful observer of the various phenomena of animal magnetism declares that, in many cases, somnambulists are capable of giving an electric shock. Mademoiselle Emmerich, a beautiful and accomplished lady, sister to Professor Emmerich, a theologian at Strasburg, became unnerved by a fright that occasioned a long and peculiar illness. According to Dr. Ennemoser, her body became so highly electrical that she imparted shocks to all who approached her bedside. Wishing to call the attention of her brother to herself on one occasion, when *he was in another part of the house*, she sent him a severe shock by the mere force of the will. Some years ago a man and his wife, living in Providence, Rhode Island, became deranged at the same time, on the subject of spiritualism. They were people who, in their best days, were susceptible and subject to impressions; they became 'mediums,' overtaxed their nervous energies, and at last went mad. They were confined in different rooms of the same house. Each was able to make impressions on the other, and each seemed to be conscious of the other's movements and feelings. . . .

"I have found, among old English ghost-stories, nothing more remarkable than 'The Haunted House in Stockwell.' The circumstances of the Stockwell wonder, which I gather from an authentic, candid, and circumstantial narrative of the astonishing transactions at Stockwell, in the county of Surrey, on Monday and Tuesday, the sixth and seventh days of January, 1772, published with the consent and approbation of the family, are as follows: On the morning of the sixth of January, 1772, Mrs. Golding, an estimable English lady, was in her parlor, when she heard the glass in her kitchen falling and breaking. She was immediately summoned to the place by her maid, who told her that the dishes were falling from the shelves. Soon after these disturbances violent noises were heard all over the house, followed by a work of destruction fearful to behold. An alarm was given that called together the neighbors, and Mr. Rowlidge, a carpenter, declared that the foundation of the house was giving way, and that the house itself was in danger of falling. The disturbances seemed to follow the maid, who gave the appearance of being perplexed and grieved, but not in the least alarmed Once, when she was called to come down from her chamber, whither she doubtless went to escape observation, she answered indifferently, and made her appearance 'without any seeming fearful apprehensions.' It became necessary to bleed Mrs. Golding. Soon after the bleeding, the blood sprung out of the basin, and the basin broke to pieces. It was thought best to remove the furniture to a neighbor's, but, whenever any valuable was taken for the purpose, it immediately went to destruction. Mr. Hames attempted to take away a costly pier-glass, but parts of the frame flew off in his hands. Mr. Saville was asked to drink some wine, but the bottle broke before it was uncorked. 'At all times of action,' says the narrative, 'Mrs. Golding's servant was walking backward and forward. Nor could they get her to sit down five minutes together, except when the family were at prayers, then all was quiet; but, in the midst of the greatest confusion, she was as much composed as at any other time, and, with uncommon coolness of temper, advised her mistress not to be alarmed or uneasy, as she said these things could not be helped.

"Mrs. Golding left her house, and, with her maid, went to Mrs. Pain's, where they passed the night. Here the work of destruction began anew. 'Everything,' says the narrative, 'was broke, till there was not above two or three cups and saucers remaining out of a considerable quantity of china.' 'About five o'clock Tuesday morning,' continues the account, 'Mrs. Golding went up to her niece and desired her to get up, as the noises and destruction were so great she could continue in the house no longer. At this time, all the tables, chairs, and drawers were tumbling about. When Mrs. Pain came down, it was amazing beyond all description. Their only security was to quit the house.' They went to a Mr Fowler's. They had barely arrived, when utensils began to fly about as before. Mr. Fowler desired Mrs. Golding to quit the house, which she did, returning to her own home. It was observed that these disturbances seemed to be in some manner connected with the maid. They followed her wherever she went, and never manifested themselves except when she was present. It was, moreover, noticed that she seemed to understand the phenomena, and to speak of them *in a familiar way*. She was a blameless girl; her mistress pitied her, but felt it her duty to discharge her. At Mrs. Golding's were broke three pailfuls of china, etc. At Mrs. Pain's the broken dishes filled two pails.

"That many remarkable effects, produced by so-called spirit-mediums, are electrical, no observant person can doubt. William Howitt, the most respectable writer on modern spiritualism, says, 'How often have we seen fire streaming from the finger of a medium! How often have we felt the touch of spirit-fingers prick as from sparks of electricity!'

"There are certain *places*, as well as persons, that become so electrical as to produce phenomena. As rapid motion develops electricity, windy and falling weather may produce it in great quantities. Dr. Livingstone mentions that the hot wind of Southern Africa is so electric that a bunch of ostrich-feathers, held against it, becomes as strongly charged as if attached to an electric machine. A gusty fall of snow on mountainous places sometimes produces so great an amount of electricity as to cause a hissing sound in the air, and to affect the hair of the traveler. The faculty of second-sight, possessed by the Highlanders of Scotland, has been attributed to certain electrical influences that abound in those hilly regions. Many phenomena once regarded as supernatural are now explained as the effects of unusual quantities of electricity generated in the atmosphere."

Mr. Butterworth cites a number of instances where similar manifestations have occurred, in which *locality*, rather than a person, seemed to furnish the requisite conditions; and those desirous of still further pursuing the subject are referred to his article in *Appletons' Journal*, vol. iv., pp. 585–6.

Enough has now been produced to exhibit many ways in which involuntary movements may occur without the aid of hypothetical "spirits." The larger portion of the more common manifestations abounding in our towns and villages may be resolved by the principles herein set forth. The involuntary powers of the mind may, without consciousness, produce any movement of the limbs or other bodily organs, possible to conscious volition. Furthermore, as in certain unhealthy states of the nervous system the unconscious action of the brain often surpasses in intellectual power the conscious action ; so it would seem that the involuntary or ideo-motor actions are often beyond the capacity of the individual to accomplish in the normal state.* Illustrations have also been

---

* In the *Springfield* (Mass.) *Republican* of a recent date, among the Vermont items, I find the following illustration of the above:

"An eleven-year-old miss named Houghton, who has received no instruction in dancing, has been mystifying Londonderry. She goes into a kind of trance, during which she trips it for hours with *no apparent effort of the will*, and with no sense of weariness, the movement and time being described as graceful and perfect."

K*

given of the occurrence of phenomena as remarkable as any furnished by the advocates of the New Dispensation, in which ponderable bodies have been moved without personal contact, and in which physical effects have been experienced, arising from a cause not under volitional direction, in which "spirit-influence" was unthought of, and not claimed by the operating force. Having prepared the way for a more critical study of modern manifestations, so loudly asserted to furnish "demonstrative evidence of the *soul's* immortality," we will venture to examine them more in detail.

2. *Hints towards a solution.*

In the winter of 1870-71, while residing in the village of Montpelier, Vt., I was introduced to a young man named Henry Allen, well known as a *medium* for physical manifestations. I attended several private *séances*, and, anxious to investigate the subject under the most favorable circumstances, invited him to my house, where an exhibition of his wonderful powers took place before about forty of my friends and neighbors. As these "manifestations" were submitted to a rigorous scrutiny, and were sufficiently marvelous to stand as a sample of the phenomena so frequently occurring, I will describe them. Mr. Allen, more widely known as "The Allen Boy," had but few preliminaries to arrange. Three large-back chairs were placed side by side across one corner of the room, facing the company assembled. Over the backs of these chairs was hung a heavy shawl, to prevent the light from the lamp from shining too brightly on the spirital scene of operations.

In this corner, behind the extemporized screen, were placed two wooden chairs, on which were laid a dulcimer, a guitar, a triangle, and I think one or two other instruments. The *medium* sat in one of the three large chairs, with his back to the instruments. The audience had carefully examined the instruments before they were placed in readiness for the expected invisible guests, and, on suggestion of Mr. Allen that a committee be appointed, selected a gentleman who was at that time a member of the State government, and was not a believer in the spirital theory. He sat down on one of the chairs adjoining Mr. Allen, and grasped his right arm with both hands, —one placed near the shoulder, the other on the wrist. Having satisfied himself that he had Mr. Allen securely by the arm, a shawl was thrown over their arms thus connected, as the "spirits" insisted it was a requisite condition to have the medium's arm and the instruments in the dark. With the light partially turned down, but not so much but that every object was visible in the room, we patiently awaited the promised manifestations. A lady kindly volunteered to sing and play on the organ to render the company harmonious, or, as I should prefer to express it, to induce the requisite state of *passivity*.

Nearly an hour elapsed before the "spirits" reported themselves. The manifestations then commenced by slight vibrations of the strings of the guitar and dulcimer, gradually increasing in power. Soon tunes were played, and the guitar was seen to rise in the air until all of it was visible except the keys, which remained in the shade. While in this position, several pieces were neatly executed. Sounds were also heard during the evening in imitation of sawing wood, boring with an auger, planing a board, and clog-dancing; also a very clever imitation of the wind roaring through the rigging of a vessel was performed on the dulcimer. A slate and pencil were passed over the backs of the chairs into the corner, *were taken*, and soon returned with writing on it purporting to be from a negro sailor drowned at sea. *Hands* frequently came in sight, sometimes pulling the hair or boxing the ears of the *medium* or of the gentleman holding him. Whenever an attempt was made to look over the screen, the phenomena ceased, and began again gradually; and, generally, after each performance the instrument was heard to drop. The slate was dropped when it was the second time passed over after being taken. When any article fell to the floor, it was not used again. At the close of the *séance* all the instruments were thrown to the floor, and the wooden chairs hurled over the large chairs into the centre of the room. A heavy arm-chair, adjoining that in which our "committee" sat, seemed exhilarated at this scene, and slowly and sedately rose several feet in the air, coming down, however, with considerable force. During most of the time Mr. Allen was employed in whistling, and the gentleman by him was frequently asked if he still retained a firm hold on his arm, and as often replied that he was unable to discover any movement on his part. His feet and limbs, as well as his head, were distinctly visible to every one in the room, and none saw any movement in the least suspicious. All the manifestations were within a radius of about five feet of the medium; most of them being between three and four feet distant. The believers were all satisfied, and the only ground for dissatisfaction on the part of the skeptical arose from their inability to account for the phenomena on any theory of their own. I was firmly convinced of the honesty of Henry Allen, and have never seen any reason to change that opinion, although familiar with what was termed an "exposé" of his powers, occurring in an Eastern city. A conviction that he *could not* have performed these wonderful feats would be justly regarded as but poor evidence; but we were all thoroughly convinced that he *did not* aid them by muscular exertion.

Here were "manifestations" enough to satisfy the most incredulous that they were not a delusion nor the result of adroit trickery. Why not then accept the spirital theory that they were the result of the presence of "spirits," as asserted by the writing on the slate? For various reasons I regard this conclusion as untenable. I had attended a number of his *séances*, and, by closely questioning those still more familiar with them, I arrived at certain conclusions, which, while not serving to explain the manner in which they were performed, were yet sufficient to discredit the alleged theory of their cause. I observed that in all his *séances* there was a general sameness. The "spirit" played the same tunes, exhibited the same phenomena, and wrote about the same meagre account of himself, night after night, with provoking monotony. Any attempt to converse by means of the slate was futile; no information could be obtained beyond the established formula reiterated on every new occasion. The seafaring "influence" seemed to be playing a part, outside of which he could not depart. If an individual "out of the form" was really the producer of these singular phenomena, and could handle the pencil to write his name and manner of his death on a slate, as well as play on the various instruments furnished, why should he not be able to answer an unexpected question or communicate other than the routine phrases? If the intelligence manifested was an unconscious manifestation of the mental powers of the *medium*, there would be no marvel in the constant reiteration of the same story. Allen, himself honestly convinced of the "spirit's" existence, would not seek to coin the answers to new questions when first presented. Allen had considerable musical talent, was familiar with the instruments used, and could whistle an accompaniment to the tunes played; and I do not believe he ever heard his hypothetical "sailor friend" play a tune entirely new to himself. Again, I observed that when any delay occurred, as frequently happened, Allen was the only one who could at once divine the cause. His inquiry was always answered with affirmative raps, whether it was for more or for less music from the organ. This mental sympathy between the *medium* and the "influence" was quite remarkable, on the spirital hypothesis.

If the intelligence shown was not of a character, then, to justify us in conceding the presence of disembodied beings, did not the physical manifestations, occurring beyond the reach of the *medium's* arm, even if he had had its use, "demonstrate" the fact that invisible beings were at work in their production? How otherwise *can* they be accounted for? exclaims the spiritist; strangely forgetting that the burden of proof rests on him, and not on those who are content with a verdict of "not proven." If he asserts that such phenomena *cannot* occur by other means, we may take exceptions to the sweeping statement, and show that they have occurred when "spirit power" was not alleged and was uncalled for.

The recent experiments undertaken by Mr. Crookes, F.R.S., Dr. Huggins, F.R.S. and a Vice-President of the Royal Society, and Mr. Cox, S.L., F.R.G.S., to determine the nature of the phenomena presented by the *medium* Home, have been narrated in most of our leading journals, and are undoubtedly familiar to the reader's mind. Mr. Serjeant Cox has recently issued a small work on the subject, entitled "Spiritualism Answered by Science," in which he holds that the experiments made have already definitely settled the question. It is not to be inferred, however that this work, of Mr. Cox, represents the views of Mr. Crookes or Dr. Huggins, neither of whom would probably coincide with many of the conclusions arrived at by their legal friend. After somewhat closely examining the results of recent investigations of the phenomena presented, a brief examination will be made of Mr. Cox's theory of psychic force, a force directed by an "entity" or "non-corporeal something" within us, and operating on matter without.

In the year 1869 the London Dialectical Society appointed a committee to examine " the asserted phenomena of spiritualism." A sub-committee, composed of persons of good social standing and intellectual abilities, proceeded to experimentally test the phenomena, not to ascertain causes or to hazard theories, but to examine and narrate results. This Society published a report of their committee in 1871, with detailed accounts of the various experiments made and phenomena witnessed. This work* presents us with many instances of so-called "physical manifestations" and mental phenomena, which would not appear in the least marvelous to one acquainted with the phenomena presented by mental pathology; but space forbids any extended reference to its contents. The report of the sub-committee No. 1 is too important, however, to be omitted; and I here present it entire:

"Since their appointment on the 16th February, 1869, your sub-committee have held *forty* meetings for the purpose of experiment and test.

"All of these meetings were held at the private resi-

---

* Report on Spiritualism of the Committee of the London Dialectical Society, together with the Evidence, Oral and Written, and a Selection from the Correspondence. London: Longman, Green, Reader & Dyer, 1871. 8vo, pp. 412.

dences of members of the committee, purposely to preclude the possibility of pre-arranged mechanism or contrivance.

"The furniture of the room in which the experiments were conducted was on every occasion its accustomed furniture.

"The tables were in all cases heavy dining-tables, requiring a strong effort to move them. The smallest of them was five feet nine inches long by four feet wide, and the largest nine feet three inches long and four and a half feet wide, and of proportionate weight.

"The rooms, tables, and furniture generally were repeatedly subjected to careful examination before, during, and after the experiments, to ascertain that no concealed machinery, instrument, or other contrivance existed by means of which the sounds or movements hereinafter mentioned could be caused.

"The experiments were conducted in the light of gas, except on the few occasions specially noted in the minutes.

"Your committee have avoided the employment of professional or paid mediums, the mediumship being that of members of your sub-committee, persons of good social position and of unimpeachable integrity, having no pecuniary object to serve, and nothing to gain by deception.

"Your committee have held some meetings without the aid of a medium (it being understood throughout this report the word 'medium' is used simply to designate an individual without whose presence the phenomena described either do not occur at all, or with greatly diminished force and frequency), purposely to try if they could produce, by any efforts, effects similar to those witnessed when a medium was present. By no endeavors were they enabled to produce anything at all resembling the manifestations which took place in the presence of a medium.

"Every test that the combined intelligence of your committee could devise has been tried with patience and perseverance. The experiments were conducted under a great variety of conditions, and ingenuity has been exerted in devising plans by which your committee might verify their observations and preclude the possibility of imposture or of delusion.

"Your committee have confined their report to *facts* witnessed by them in their collective capacity, which facts were palpable to the senses, and their *reality* capable of demonstrative proof.

"Of the members of your sub-committee about four-fifths entered upon the investigation wholly skeptical as to the reality of the alleged phenomena, firmly believing them to be the result either of *imposture* or of *delusion*, or of *involuntary muscular action*. It was only by irresistible evidence under conditions that precluded the possibility of either of these solutions, and after trial and test many times repeated, that the most skeptical of your sub-committee were slowly and reluctantly convinced that the phenomena exhibited in the course of their protracted inquiry *were veritable facts*.

"The result of their long-continued and carefully-conducted experiments, after trial by every detective test they could devise, has been to establish *conclusively:*

"First. That, under certain *bodily or mental* conditions of one or more of the persons present, a force is exhibited sufficient to set in motion heavy substances, without the employment of any muscular force, without contact or material connection of any kind between such substances and the body of any person present.

"Second. That this force can cause sounds to proceed, distinctly audible to all present, from solid substances not in contact with, nor having any visible or material connection with, the body of any person present, and which sounds are proved to proceed from such substances by the vibrations which are distinctly felt when they are touched.

"Third. That this force is frequently directed by intelligence.

"At thirty-four out of the forty meetings of your committee some of these phenomena occurred.

"A description of one experiment, and the manner of conducting it, will best show the care and caution with which your committee have pursued their investigations.

"So long as there was contact, or even the possibility of contact, by the hands or feet, or even by the clothes, of any person in the room, with the substance moved or sounded, there could be no perfect assurance that the motions and sounds were not produced by the person so in contact. The following experiment was therefore tried:

"On an occasion when eleven members of your sub-committee had been sitting round one of the dining-tables above described for forty minutes, and various motions and sounds had occurred, they, by way of test, turned the backs of their chairs to the table, at about nine inches from it. They all then knelt upon their chairs, placing their arms upon the backs thereof. In this position, their feet were of course turned away from the table, and by no possibility could be placed under it or touch the floor. The hands of each person were extended over the table at about four inches from the surface. Contact, therefore, with any part of the table could not take place without detection.

"In less than a minute the table, untouched, moved *four* times; at first about *five* inches to one side, then about *twelve* inches to the opposite side, and then in like manner four inches and six inches respectively.

"The hands of all present were next placed on the backs of their chairs, and about a foot from the table, which again moved as before, *five* times, over spaces varying from four to six inches. Then all the chairs were removed twelve inches from the table, and each person knelt on his chair as before; this time, however, folding his hands behind his back, his body being thus about eighteen inches from the table, and having the back of the chair between himself and the table. The table again moved *four* times, in various directions. In the course of this conclusive experiment, and in less than half an hour, the table thus moved, without contact or possibility of contact with any person present, *thirteen* times, the movements being in different directions, and some of them according *to the request* of various members of your sub-committee.

"The table was then carefully examined, turned upside down, and taken to pieces, but nothing was discovered to account for the phenomena. The experiment was conducted throughout in the full light of gas above the table.

"Altogether, your sub-committee have witnessed upwards of *fifty* similar motions without contact, on *eight* different evenings, in the houses of members of your sub-committee, the most careful tests being applied on each occasion.

"In all similar experiments the possibility of mechanical or other contrivance was further negatived by the fact that the movements were in various directions,—now to one side, then to the other; now up the room, now down the room: motions that would have required the co-operation of many hands or feet; and these, from the great size and weight of the tables, could not have been so used without the visible exercise of muscular force. Every hand and foot was plainly to be seen, and could not have been moved without instant detection.

"Delusion was out of the question. The motions were in various directions, and were witnessed simultaneously by all present. They were matters of *measurement*, and not of opinion or of fancy.

"And they occurred so often, under so many and such various conditions, with such safeguards against error or deception, and with such invariable results, as to satisfy the members of your sub-committee by whom the experiments were tried, wholly skeptical as most of them were when they entered upon the investigation, that *there is a force capable of moving heavy bodies without material contact, and which force is in some unknown manner dependent upon the presence of human beings.*

"Your sub-committee have not, collectively, obtained any evidence as to the nature and source of this force, but simply as to the *fact of its existence.*

"There appears to your committee to be no ground for the popular belief that the presence of skeptics interferes in any manner with the production or action of the force.

"In conclusion, your committee express their unanimous opinion that the one important physical fact thus proved to exist, that motion may be produced in solid bodies without material contact, by some hitherto unrecognized force operating within an undefined distance from the human organism, and beyond the range of muscular action, should be subjected to further scientific examination, with a view to ascertain its true source, nature, and power.

"The notes of the experiments made at each meeting of your sub-committee are appended to this report."

Mr. Serjeant Cox, a member of this sub-committee, in his work referred to above, supplements these experiments with some additional ones witnessed by himself elsewhere, a few of which are herewith presented. The first may justly be termed a "*striking* manifestation."

"The next experiment was with the same psychic (*medium*), in the house of Dr. Edmunds, with a dining-table of unusual weight and size. The same test, by turning the backs of the chairs to the table and the experimentalists kneeling upon them, produced the same results, but to a much greater extent than we had before witnessed. In that position of the entire party, a heavy dining-table moved six times,—once over a space of eight inches at a swing. Then all the party, holding hands, stood in a circle round the table, at the distance from it first of two feet, and then of three feet, so that contact by any person present was physically impossible. In this position the table lurched four times,—once over a space of *more than two feet*, and with great force. The extent of these movements without contact will be understood when I state that in the course of them this ponderous table *turned completely round;* that is to say, the end that was at the top of the room when the experiment began was at the bottom of the room when it concluded. The most remarkable part of this experiment was the finale. The table had been turned to within two feet of a complete reversal of its first position, and was standing out of square with the room. The party had broken up, and were gathered in groups about the room. Suddenly the table was swung violently over the two feet of distance between its then position and its proper place, and set exactly square with the room, *literally knocking down a lady* who was standing in the way, in the act of putting on her shawl for departure. At that time *nobody was touching the table,* nor even within reach of it, except the young lady who was knocked down by it. . . .

"Alterations in the weight of tables and other furniture have been frequently exhibited. Bidding the table to be light, a finger lifted it; the next moment, bidding it to be heavy, the entire force of the body was required to raise it from the floor. It was, however, suggested, by myself and others who were engaged in the *scientific* investigation of the phenomena of psychic force, that possibly this change in the weight of the subject of the force might be merely in our own sensations, and not an actual change in the gravity of the wood, or the operation of any pressure upon it. To test this, a weighing machine was constructed, with a hook to fix to the table, the index accurately marking the weight of whatever was attached to it. Applying this machine to the table and other bodies, we found that the change was really in them, and not sensational merely, as we had suspected. This simple experiment was tried so often, and with so many precautions, as to establish it beyond doubt. The weights varied at every trial, but all proved the reality of the force that was operating. One instance will suffice. Weighed by the machine, the normal weight of a table, raised from the floor eighteen inches on one side, was eight pounds; desired to be light, the index fell to five pounds; desired to be heavy, it advanced to eighty-two pounds; and these changes were instantaneous and repeated many times.

"Not only is motion communicated to the table or other article of furniture, where the psychic is, but everything within some definite, though as yet undefined, distance from the psychic appears to be subjected to the force. The smaller furniture of the room is frequently attracted to the place at which the psychic sits. Chairs, far out of reach and untouched, may be seen moving along the floor in a manner singularly resembling the motion that may be observed in pieces of steel attracted by a magnet, which rise a little, fall, move on, stop, until fully within the influence of the magnetic force, and then jump to the magnet with a sudden spring. The chairs, that are so often seen to come across the room to the psychic, usually approach by irregular motions, gliding for a short space, stopping, moving, and so on, until fully within the influence, and then the last movement is by a rapid jump. Larger articles of furniture are attracted in like manner, according to weight; chairs more easily the whole length of a large room; a sofa will advance two feet or three feet only. Plainly the force is limited in power. It can move only a certain *weight;* bulk is no impediment to its exercise. Nor is this phenomenon at all dubious to the spectator. It cannot be fanciful; it is not a delusion. However it may be done, the *fact* is indisputable that it *is* done. The chairs start from the wall against which they are placed; the sofa rolls forward; the smaller tables approach. This occurs in the light of gas, in the private room of any person who makes trial of it, is seen by all, and often gives inconvenient proof of the fact by encompassing the seated circle. At one experiment six drawing-room chairs were attracted from the other side of the room, over distances ranging from six feet to ten feet, and thrust themselves against the circle; two large easy-chairs advanced three feet; and a large settee advanced about two feet. No person was near either of them. In another experiment in my own lighted drawing-room, as the psychic was entering the door with myself, no *other person being there,* an easy-chair, of great weight, that was standing fourteen feet from us, was suddenly lifted from the floor, and drawn to him with great rapidity, precisely as a huge magnet would attract a mass of iron."

A physician, of high standing in his profession, residing in an Eastern city, informs me that eighteen years ago he devoted considerable attention to the phenomenon of table-turning, and with such success that, after the movement of the table had commenced, he could direct it to move in any direction, without contact, the table obeying his will as if it possessed an animate existence. During my experiments with the planchette, one instance occurred of the movement of the little instrument when no hand was resting on it. It had written the name of a deceased friend of a gentleman present, and had repeatedly written the word "music." The gentleman stepped out of the room into another to gratify the wish, and while the sounds of the organ were heard the planchette, though untouched, appeared to be *dancing* on the table. We had been asking for "spirit-communications," and received what would be termed a veritable "test." Was it indeed so?

Dr. Carpenter, in a recent lecture, speaking of table-turning, says, "It was found that the table would tilt in obedience to the direction of some spirit, who was in the first instance (I speak now of about *twenty* years ago) always believed to be an evil spirit. The table-tilting first developed itself in Bath, under the guidance of some clergymen there, who were quite satisfied that the tiltings of the table were due to the presence of evil spirits. And one of these clergymen went further, and said it was Satan himself. But it was very curious that the answers obtained by the rappings and tiltings *always followed the notions* of the persons who put the questions. These clergymen always got their answers as from evil spirits, or satisfied themselves that they were evil spirits by the answers they got. But, on the other hand, other persons got answers of a different kind; an innocent girl, for instance, asked the table if it loved her, and the table jumped up and kissed her."

The report made to the Dialectical Society presents us with a striking illustration of the above. A gentleman, claiming to have had seventeen years' experience of the phenomenon in question, gave his testimony before the committee. He said, "On one occasion, the answer given to the inquiry being obviously untrue, the witness peremptorily inquired why a correct answer had not been given, and the spirit in reply said, 'Because I am Beelzebub!'

"One day the table turned at right angles, and went into the corner of the room. I asked, 'Are you my child?' but obtained no answer. I then said, 'Are you from God?' but the table was still silent. I then said, 'In the name of the Father, Son, and Holy Spirit, I *command* you to answer. Are you from God?' One loud rap—a negative—was then given. 'Do you believe,' said I, 'that Christ died to save us from sin?' The answer was, 'No!' '*Accursed spirit,*' said I, 'leave the room.' The table then walked across the room, entered the adjoining one, and quickened its steps. It was a small tripod table. It walked with a sidelong walk. It went to the door, shook the handle, and I opened it. The table walked into the passage, and I repeated the adjuration, receiving *the same answer*. Finally, *convinced* that I was dealing with an accursed spirit, I opened the street-door, and the table was immediately silent; no movement or rap was heard. I returned alone to the drawing-room, and asked if there were any spirits present. Immediately I heard steps like those of a little child outside the door. I opened it, and the small table went into the corner as before, just as my child did when I reproved it for a fault. These manifestations continued until I used the adjuration, and I always found that they changed or ceased when the name of God was mentioned. One night, when sitting alone in my drawing-room, I heard a noise at the top of the house. A servant who had heard it came into the room frightened. I went to the nursery, and found that the sounds came from a spot near the bed.* I pronounced the adjuration, and they instantly ceased. The same sounds were afterwards heard in the kitchen, and I succeeded in restoring quiet as before.

"Reflecting on these singular facts, I determined to inquire further, and really satisfy myself that the manifestations were what I suspected them to be. I went to Mrs. Marshall, and took with me three clever men, who were not at all likely to be deceived. I was quite unknown. We sat at a table, and had a *séance*. Mrs. Marshall told me the name of my child. I asked the spirit some questions, and then pronounced the adjuration. We all heard steps which sounded as if some one were mounting the wall: in a few seconds the sound ceased, and, although Mrs. Marshall challenged again and again, the spirit did not answer, and she could not account for the phenomenon. In this case I pronounced the adjuration mentally; no person knew what I had done. At a *séance* held at the house of a friend of mine at which I was present, manifestations were obtained; and, as I was *known to be hostile*, I was entreated not to interfere. I sat for two hours a *passive* spectator. I then asked the name of the spirit, and it gave that of my child. 'In the name of the

---

* "A child is usually a more powerful psychic than a man."—Cox, p. 53.

Father, Son, and Holy Ghost,' said I, 'are you the spirit of my child?' It answered, 'No!' and the word '*devil*' was spelled out.

"My opinion of these phenomena is that the intelligence which is put in communication with us is a fallen one. It is of the devil, the prince of the power of the air. I believe that we commit the crime of necromancy when we take part in these spiritual *séances*.

"At the Spiritual Athenæum I saw written up as a motto the words, ' Try the spirits.' I did so, and found that they were not from God. Of course I believe in the New Testament. Any spirit which denies the atonement or does not believe in the Trinity cannot be from God. When we pronounce the name of God, we must mean what St. John meant, the three persons in one."

To this account of personal experience the witness somewhat naïvely adds, " I have never stopped them by an effort of the will alone.(!) I never used the adjuration without stopping the manifestations."

The general committee of the Dialectical Society comprised thirty-four persons, including scientific and literary, professional and business men, and their report may be briefly summed up as follows :

1. Solid substances may be set in motion without muscular exertion or personal contact, and, in obedience to an expressed desire from persons present, will move in a required direction.

2. Sounds may be heard proceeding from furniture, floors, walls, and other solid substances, and vibrations accompanying the sounds are distinctly felt.

3. By means of these movements and sounds coherent communications can be spelled out, though the intelligence manifested never rises above a commonplace character.

4. Facts generally unknown are frequently revealed in this manner, yet are always known to at least *one* person present.

5. The power by which these phenomena occur evidently proceeds from the human organism.

(To the above may be appended these additional conclusions, as legitimate deductions from the facts set forth in the preceding pages:)

6. The character of the intelligence is determined by the convictions of those present.

In the case of the spiritist, it is spirits of the dead; with the believer in demoniacal possession, it is of the devil; with the unbiased scientific investigator, it is simply intelligence, making no claim to distinct personality. And, furthermore, it may be confidently laid down that if a circle were composed of individuals whose minds were filled with a conviction of the existence of fairyland, fairies and elves would be as ready to respond (or "commune") as Tom Scrubbs to the spiritists, or Beelzebub to superstitious inquirers.

7. This force frequently proceeds from persons who are not believers in spirit-communion.

It is sometimes manifested when the object of the *séance* is to prove that "spirits" are not essential to its manifestation, thus compelling the spiritist to assume the paradox that the skeptical *medium controls* the "spirit" to give *tests* that "spirits" are not concerned in the manifestation! Of the *medium* employed by the sub-committee of the Dialectical Society, whose report has been given, Mr. Cox says that, after resolving that no professional *medium* should be employed, "a psychic was found in the person of a lady, the wife of one of the members of the general committee, of high professional and social position. In this we were pre-eminently fortunate; for the lady in question had never witnessed any of the phenomena with others, and therefore could not have mastered the sleight of hand, requiring the practice of a life for its mastery, which would be necessary for the successful performance of a trick, if trick it was. In truth, she had discovered their production in her own presence only by chance, a few weeks previously to acceding to the request of the sub-committee to assist them in their investigations."

8. The *medium* is an unconscious agent.

Not an agent, however, in the hands of a hypothetical "influence." Exercising no power of the will over the manifestation of this force, a *passive* condition of mind is induced in the *medium*, and the dominant thought or feeling gives rise to and shapes the actions performed; these manifestations occur more markedly, however, in the presence of others in like passive moods than when alone.

9. This force is variable in its manifestation.

At one moment slight and tremulous, in the next powerful and rapid. It is affected by all the *physical* conditions affecting the physical condition of the *medium*, such as atmospheric changes, higher or lower temperatures, his or her nervous condition or that of others present: in short, whatever tends to weaken the *nerve-energy* of the *medium* will lessen the flow of the force, and *vice versa*. Rarely manifested immediately, a certain time is generally spent in awaiting the phenomena, during which nothing must occur to impair the complete *passivity* of the mind; and this brings us to the final conclusion.

10. "Physical manifestations" are the result of a nerve-force proceeding from the human organism, under the control of the unconscious workings of the mind, by some process not as yet clearly defined by science.

Mr. Cox, in commenting on the phenomena witnessed by the committee of which he was a member, says, "So far as I have found in my own experience, and by the reported experience of others, it appears that the intelligence of the communication is measured by the intelligence of the psychic. Nothing is conveyed by them that is not in the mind of the psychic or of some person present.

"There is nothing in the character or substance of the communications indicating an intelligence higher than our own, or a larger knowledge. They are often useless and purposeless; they are rarely absolute nonsense; but as rarely do they exhibit anything beyond ordinary intelligence. They consist mainly of moral platitudes; both the thought and the language reflect the thoughts and language of the psychic.

"Not unfrequently the communications are false in point of fact. They are often tentative, as if the directing intelligence had an imperfect perception of the object or subject, or as if it were guessing rather than knowing the answer to be given. The descriptions of the future life are precisely such as the psychic would form. By a child psychic they are painted according to a child's notions of heaven; and when the psychic is a man or a woman, they are described in accordance with the particular conceptions of a heaven entertained by that psychic. These differences as to the process of death and the conditions of a future life prove that the descriptions do not proceed from any intelligence actually acquainted with them, and therefore *not* from the spirits of the dead."

Mr. Cox here sets forth in a few words the impression derived from a year and a half's scientific investigation of "spirit-communion;" but those who have read with attention the preceding chapters will be prepared to admit that under mental exaltation the intelligence evinced may be far superior to the normal mental capacity of the medium, and, furthermore, that, when susceptible to mental impressions, facts long forgotten—or "out of mind"— may be recalled by hearing them from the medium's lips. But such instances are very rare even among *mediums*. The commonplace character of the messages observed in England is also to be plainly discerned in this country, as well as the connection existing between the *ideas* of the medium and that written as a "message." A gentleman residing in Lowell, Mass., visited a "test-medium," and received as a "test," supposed to "demonstrate" an endless amount of speculation, the name of "T. Pane" written in blood-red letters on the bared arm of the medium. Hardly prepared to believe that Paine had forgotten how to spell his own name, he accepted the phenomenon as a "test," though not in the manner designed. He subsequently ascertained that the *medium* was a very illiterate person.

I have now before me two "spirit-messages" written by Mr. Charles Foster, who, at the time they were written, 1866, enjoyed the reputation of being the most powerful and convincing "test-medium" in this country. I visited him, paid one dollar, and for value received brought away these lines, heralded with the due amount of rappings and table-tiltings. The first is from a comrade who fell in battle in my presence:

"This is a pleasure for me to come here to-night as an evidence of spirit-communion. I am ever by your *side*, watching over *you*, and wish you to fully realize my presence. The time is not far distant when you will have a full vision of your unseen friends; we are working

now to that end, to bring about such evidences through you as will convince you *beyond* a doubt of our presence.
"CHARLEY ———."

—omitting the initials of two middle names, as well as certain information I was desirous of obtaining, and which he could have given if he indited the above. The second is from a deceased aunt, of whom I had not been thinking, but whose name had been written on a slip of paper by Mr. Foster, who said she desired to "communicate." I accordingly wrote on paper the following: "Can you write or speak any message you desire to give?" In response the following lines were written underneath:

"I am here to prove that we are working for you from the spirit-life. I come to you *uncalled* for, and wish to bear you a message of love from the heavenly *world* to assure you of my presence. Sit often, and you will be refreshed. "SARAH ———."

The signature is written in what purports to be a *fac-simile* of the deceased's handwriting; but to this "message" she has appended her name in accordance with the modern mode of spelling the Christian name. Her name was Sally; she was so christened, so called, and it is so inscribed on her tombstone.

Reader, our companionship is now drawing to a close. In our investigation of the phenomena accredited to spiritual beings, we have seen that they fail to afford demonstrative evidence of such origin. On the contrary, a rigid scrutiny reveals a close similarity to phenomena of which the origin is to be sought in the laws of mental physiology and pathology. Having traced this power, in mental phenomena, to mental exaltation, or to unconscious action of the brain, and in physical manifestations, to its seat in the nervous system, we may dismiss from our minds all further consideration of so-called "demonstrations of spirit-communion." But one question remains, which will undoubtedly arise in every mind. Having shown that a force exists, emanating from the nervous system of human beings, what can be said in regard to its *nature* and *methods* of acting? The temptation has been very great with all writers against the spirital theory to endeavor to explain in just what manner all the various phenomena may be accounted for. Each one, from the Buffalo M.D.'s in 1848, to Serjeant Cox in 1872, has had a *theory* to offer, but which, unfortunately, has invariably failed to meet all the requirements of the *facts*.

Mr. Cox, the most recent theorist on this subject, has given to the public many valuable facts, but in his *inferences* from them I think he has transcended the limits of scientific inquiry. In his preface he states:

"The crucial tests applied by the skill and science of Mr. Crookes confirmed the result of a series of other experiments, conducted with care and caution, which had been instituted for the purpose of investigating if any and what of the alleged phenomena were real; and, if real, whether they are physical or spiritual, natural or supernatural.

"The conclusion from that patient inquiry has been, that many of the alleged phenomena are real, though some are delusions and others impostures; that the power dignified by the title of spiritual, because attributed to the presence and action of spirits of the dead, is in fact a psychic force proceeding from the human structure and directed by the human intelligence.

"But from what part of the human structure that force

proceeds,—whether from nerve, ganglion, or brain,—if it be the vital force, or 'nerve-ether' of Dr. Richardson, if the directing intelligence is the 'unconscious cerebration' of Dr. Carpenter, or if there be a soul (or spirit) inhabiting the body and distinct from it, by which those effects are produced, are problems remaining for close, patient, and extensive research, by steadily pursuing the course of scientific investigation which Mr. Crookes has so successfully begun."

To this statement of the case I urge no objection; but he goes on to state further what I deem unwarranted by the facts and not in accord with science. He says:

"For theology and modern science *are directly at issue* as to the existence of a soul in man. Theology affirms, and science either denies or doubts, demanding proofs. If psychic force be the reality that they who have scientifically examined and tested it assert, it shakes to its foundation the materialism of modern science, by the probability it raises that, *as a fact in nature*, there is in us an *entity, distinct* from the corporeal structure, which can *exercise* an active *force*, beyond the limit of the bodily powers, and which is not material, but something other than that the scalpel carves and the microscope reveals.

"The purpose of this brief treatise is to state fully and frankly the facts and arguments that have conducted to the conclusion that there *is* such a force, and a *non-corporeal* something in us that controls it, and that science may yet be enabled to restore the faith science has shaken in the existence of the soul and the consequent prospect of immortality."

Here we have the old error of the spiritist repeated. He would materialize spirit by this process of reasoning quite as much as those do whom we are criticising; an error similar in nature to that of the sublimated author of "The Hollow Globe," who says directly what in the above is logically implied, as follows: "It will be difficult to find the dividing line between physical and spiritual substances, if there be any such line, and tell where matter terminates and spirit commences, or which is matter and which is spirit." In the preceding chapter we have seen that the tendency of scientific research is to establish the correlation of all forces. In the words of Herbert Spencer, "*Any* force manifested implies an equal antecedent force from which it is derived, and against which it is a reaction." And again in another work we have seen that he states the position of science in these words: "It follows, from the persistence of force, that each portion of mechanical or *other* energy which an organism exerts implies the transformation of as much organic matter as contained this energy in a latent state." Emerson humorously says, "I knew a witty physician who found theology in the biliary duct, and used to affirm that if there was disease of the liver the man became a Calvinist, and if that organ was sound he became a Unitarian." But to urge as "a fact in nature" that the soul may be sought in a ganglion, or manifest a physical force "distinct from the corporeal structure," is unwarranted alike by sound philosophy and modern science.

I have not sought to advocate any specific *theory* with which all the phenomena will be found to accord; on the contrary, the psychological facts underlying the spiritual philosophy are various in their causes, and, while some may be classified as instances of mental exaltation or unconscious activity of the mind, others are explicable on the ground of mental sympathy, or seem to be the result oftentimes of a force proceeding from the nervous system of one or more individuals, and operating in a manner, as yet, not clearly defined. To give reasons for believing that spirits of the dead are *not* concerned in any of these various phenomena has been the object of the foregoing pages ; and however more forcibly the matter might have been presented, still if they serve to satisfy doubts existing in the minds of so many in view of the marvelousness of the phenomena witnessed, and shall lead any one to clearer conceptions of the distinction between spiritual and physical existence, the author will feel that his labor has not been in vain.

THE END

www.ingramcontent.com/pod-product-compliance
Lightning Source LLC
Chambersburg PA
CBHW020758230426
43666CB00007B/758